THIN...

AND MAKE IT HAPPEN

AT WORK

THINK CHANGE!

AND MAKE IT HAPPEN

AT WORK

Paul Sansome

RIGHT WAY

Typeset in 11/12 pt Times by Letterpart Limited, Reigate, Surrey.
Printed and bound in Great Britain by Cox & Wyman Limited, Reading, Berkshire.

The *Right Way* series is published by Elliot Right Way Books, Brighton Road, Lower Kingswood, Tadworth, Surrey, KT20 6TD, U.K. For information about our company and the other books we publish, visit our web site at www.right-way.co.uk

CONTENTS

PREFACE

At 07:30 on the morning of the 14th November 1975, a fresh-faced youth got out of his bed, *considerably earlier than he was used to*, and entered for the first time the world of business. It was fortunate for him that, having joined an industry that was probably the most dynamic in the world, he was about to be involved in it going through the most volatile twenty-year period of change in its history.

He joined the computer industry, which, in the 1970s, was hardly an industry at all. It was the province of analysts, boffins and technocrats whose members frequently sported beards and sandals and whose normal behaviour was largely indistinguishable from the irresponsible fun and frivolity enjoyed in a university research department. By the 1990s it had become a real industry; no longer run by scientists and engineers, but now managed by some of the most influential businessmen in the world. The boffins wore suits and ties, hair was cut and nails were clipped. The fun and laughter had become less frequent and more reserved. The in-office games of baseball had petered out to nothing, as had the after-work house parties. Professionalism had generally replaced passion. Partners and parenting had replaced midnight programming. Everyone had learned the rules of corporate life and how

In the 1970s it was hardly an industry at all.

to conform. In the 1990s the computer business took itself very seriously. It had to. It was an industry upon which virtually every other organisation on the planet now depended for its survival. It was an industry that had become so volatile that multi-billion dollar companies went bust in days, while others grew to replace them, in months. No longer was the industry a frivolous youth, it had grown up into a middle-aged, firmly middle-class, responsible adult.

Within two years of joining the industry his interest in the technology started to wane as he became ever more fascinated by the process of change itself and its effect upon people. He therefore moved into management and decided that what he wanted most from his career was to experience first-hand the management of change. From project management to matrix management, from central-ised authority to de-centralised autonomy, from investor in things to investors in people, from the scientific revolution to the quality revolution. Everywhere, for good or ill, he saw, led, supported and made change. He saw people managing change, coming to terms with change, enjoying and exploiting change. He saw people: ignoring change, fearing change and being overwhelmed by change. Nothing he saw was immune from change.

By 1996, he too had changed. He was no longer quite so fresh-faced or so youthful. The tummy had expanded and the hairline had contracted. But there was one change, from back in the 1970s, that he had never got used to. That was getting up at such an ungodly hour every day to go to the office.

So he left the computer industry and went back to bed, to think about the lessons he had learned from the manage-ment of change.

He started to reflect that, over the years, he observed change being supported by analysts, writers, consultants and gurus, but was increasingly puzzled by the fact that many of them appeared to make simple ideas complicated and also appeared to hate each other.

He spoke to some of these great men (no names no pack-drill) and asked them about this phenomenon. Each strongly denied that it was the case and explained that there was a healthy respect for, and professional open debate of, each other's ideas. Each made a point of empha-sising that their fellow gurus were highly talented and respected people; whereupon the individual "worthy" he was talking to would invariably, immediately and without ceremony, deliver a savage verbal dig at his nearest "rival".

It took him some time to work out what was happening.

To put it simply, he concluded that being a guru encompassed, almost by definition, a belief that one was right and a belief that one's ideas were unique. Therefore, gurus tended to make simple ideas unique by complicating them and tended to reject completely alternative thinking.

I was that fresh-faced youth back in 1975, who has been enjoying the thrills and spills of a change-ridden career ever since. Like most managers in the real world, I win a few and lose a few, sometimes getting it right and sometimes screwing-up. Never have I walked the enlightened path of the guru – and I hope I never do.

We ordinary managers (managers who actually try to run the business of our companies) are, when it comes to gurudom, free. Free of dogma. Free to agree and disagree, and applaud and criticise, all the gurus, and their disciples. We have the freedom and opportunity to find values from combining their ideas and working them in with our own to see if anything useful happens.

I am like you, a real manager who tries to make a living in the real world. I happen to have spent a large proportion of my career studying change and the reaction of people to it. I have been fortunate enough to have found out about, used, and then refined for myself, various ideas, concepts, tools and techniques that help determine which changes yield the greatest benefit and to engineer those changes with success.

There is no simple cook-book answer to the problem of making effective change to attain excellence. There is no magic wand or universal formula. Over many years, I have become convinced that the only way is to challenge and question everything in the business. To do this you must develop an open mind that is never afraid to kick against dogma, hierarchy, systems and conventional management wisdom when you believe that by doing so you will effect an improvement of value. To be this challenging within an organisation you must be trusted by your pay-masters (or suffer the consequences). Developing such trust requires you to behave with absolute integrity at all times, demonstrating again and again that your motives are solely focused upon the good of the organisation and its customers. Of course sound motives won't make you right every time. To maintain the trust means being honest. Honest with colleagues, honest with customers and, most importantly of all, being honest with yourself. Your honesty and integrity comes to the fore when you make mistakes. With no cook-book you are bound to try things that don't work. You are bound to suggest things that others will not accept. You are bound to look foolish on occasion. You are even bound to try some things that do work, only to see a queue of formerly uninvolved critics lining up to take the credit.

Managing an organisation that is constantly responsive to changes in markets, competition, technology, economy and environment is a long haul. You are not embarking upon a one-year, two-year, or even five-year strategy. You are embarking upon a fundamental lifestyle change that will affect everyone in the organisation and everything that is done in the organisation. You are attempting to develop a culture, or habit, of thinking and of making changes everywhere throughout the enterprise. Managing such a change of lifestyle, of culture and of habit, will take decades and will never be complete. For a haul of such magnitude, only your personal conviction will carry you through.

The path will be arduous with many barriers and pitfalls along the way. Time and again your energy and enthusiasm will be sapped. Time and again you will discover short-cuts which, on closer examination, you discover to be a long way round. To keep going, like any traveller, you must enjoy the journey. So pause often to take in the view and to laugh with your fellow travellers. Never take yourself too seriously. The more fun you have on the way, the more likely you are to make real progress. Remember, managing change is never-ending, so you better enjoy the trip.

I have most certainly not arrived at journey's end. I have simply stopped along the way to reflect upon my progress so far. Having left the computer industry, I am no longer constrained to get up at an ungodly hour to go to the office every day. I can, for a while, enjoy the opportunity to meditate on the lessons I have learned and to share my ideas with other travellers.

So let us rest awhile together, before you embark upon your path to responsiveness and excellence. Our discussion may just help you to enjoy the trip.

A short note on gender
In various places in this book I have referred to *he* and *him*, while in other places I have used *s/he* and similarly ugly syntactic devices. Please accept my apologies for my literary clumsiness and understand that throughout the book it is my intention to address men and women equally.

A short note on organisations
In various places in this book I have referred to *organisation, company, business* and similar epithets. Again, I must beg the reader's indulgence. I have used these terms loosely. The need to "***Think Change, and make it happen***" applies to any organisation, profit-making or otherwise, work-related or not.

1

THE FEAR FACTOR

While producing this book, Martin and I were discussing an early draft. Martin is a friend of mine who also happens to be a highly experienced and able marketing, sales and business development director of a medium-sized electronics company. I asked him if he agreed with me that few managers actually read the management books they buy and if so why this was. His answer was typical of the man: pragmatic, simple, clear and probably with more truth in it than many would admit. He said, "Of course I don't read 'em. It's simple; I do my reading in bed, not at my desk. So when I'm reading, I'm tired. Because of that, I want stories, opinions and ideas that are simple to grasp; I don't want to read a book that has facts, numbers and equations – most management tomes are just too hard on the brain. If I'm reading it in bed I want a book that I can hold in one hand – most management books are inches thick. And at night my eyes are tired, so I don't want a book whose print is so small that I need to get my specs to read it."

Inspired, I vowed that this book would be as easy to read and as chatty as I could make it. I also vowed that I would keep the length down and make sure that it was printed in slightly bigger than usual letters. At least if I did that, the book would not disappoint Martin.

Most management tomes are just too hard on the brain.

Too many of our organisations disappoint and unhappiness prevails. In far too many cases, employees are unhappy, customers are unhappy, leaders and managers are unhappy. In too many organisations the finances are disappointing, the products are disappointing and the services disappoint both the deliverer and the recipient.

Too many of our organisations have, for years, been seeking the quick fix, trying to do it now, working for instant gratification. Re-branding the same old stuff as new, re-packaging it as exciting, re-engineering it as a cure-all.

It just doesn't work. Few, if any, of us get excited about soap powder, whatever box it comes in. The "Have a nice day" brand of courtesy fools no one – indeed I would suggest that what most of us want is the old-fashioned genuine sort. The highly engineered "management methodologies" sure seem to cost a lot, promise a lot and seem impressive, but how many of them actually make a real and lasting difference?

We need a more flexible approach, one that is natural and sustainable for the long term. An approach based, not upon formulae, but upon pragmatism and human values.

This book discusses some of the ideas and principles that have worked for me, and that I have seen work for others. It starts by going back to the first principles of quality and considers the changes needed to make products that deliver that which is promised. It progresses to talk of change through customers and the development of business relationships. It then considers the management of cultural change and the design of integrated change programmes for continuous improvement and hence on towards continuous learning, re-thinking and striving for true business excellence.

This book talks about the legal "creative theft" of process benchmarking. It talks of management by evolution versus management by revolution and suggests that it is the latter that has flattened and left to rot the landscape of Britain's industrial heartland. It talks of managing for the long term. And it talks about people – people as workers, people as customers, people as managers, people as teachers, champions, trainers and coaches.

It talks too about mistakes . . .

So, how many mistakes do you make in the average day?

No, don't just read the question, really think about it. How many mistakes do you make in the average day?

No, I'm not interested in "a few," or "not many," or "goodness knows." I want you to think about it *properly*. How many? A real number.

No, I don't care how you define mistakes, do it in your own terms. How many times do you get it wrong?

Write down the number in the box here.
The number of mistakes I make in the
average day:

Now multiply this number by 365 and
write that number in the box here.
The number of times every year that I
personally screw-up:

So, how do you feel now? That's mistakes for you!

Later in the book we will discuss mistakes again and the significance of the exercise you have just done – assuming that you have actually done it . . . which of course you haven't, have you? No. You have stopped and thought about it for a few seconds, but you haven't actually written anything down, have you? You don't want to commit yourself. You are waiting until you've seen the answer in the back of the book so that you can pretend that you knew the answer all the time. That's the Fear Factor!

As managers, we enjoy a position of some authority and status. To reflect this position we arm ourselves with a firm, confident, professional exterior, and we go to great lengths to protect it. However, I think that many of us, under the surface, carry the baggage of insecurity and self-centredness. We find ourselves, too often, worrying more about keeping our own jobs than we do about helping others succeed in theirs. Too often we avoid making decisions, because that way we avoid making wrong decisions. Too often we operate in a world of confidentiality, safe in the knowledge that if no one knows what we do, then no one can know what we do wrong. We fear mistakes, are fearful of having to admit the possibility that we make them, and frightened that we might be found out.

As managers, you enjoy positions of some authority and status.

Worse, we spread these fears throughout the organisations in which we work.

We will return to mistakes later.

Many of the concepts discussed in the book are profound. Not quite up to "The Meaning of Life" level, but sometimes fairly close. Despite this, they are all fairly simple – management really isn't rocket science; in fact management is seldom more than old-fashioned, boring, common sense; which probably explains why so often it is done so badly. Common sense, after all, is noted for being the least common commodity in the world.

Many of the concepts are about people and relationships; hence they are subjective. You must therefore feel free to argue with absolutely anything you like. I have tried not to include dogmatic answers and recipes for success – you don't need patronising and, anyway, there are no guaranteed recipes.

As I said, many of the concepts in the book are simple. The profound thing is how you think about them and what you do about them. I have tried to keep them simple by avoiding, wherever I can, Techno-babble and Manager-speak. The gurus, in my observation, spend their lives packaging ideas into a form of mysticism. I am not a mystic. As for you, you've either got religion already or have decided you don't need it. In either case, you are not in the market for another one.

The ideas in this book are fundamentally about everyone questioning every feature of every part of your business. Questioning like this, and then taking action, is quite a challenge. This book and the various courses I run, as well as many other books and courses written by others are there to help you face this challenge.

Use them or not; it's up to you – but then, so is the performance of your business.

THE FEAR FACTOR
A Summary For Browsers

★ Too many organisations disappoint.
    Unhappy customers.
    Unhappy employees.
    Unhappy leaders and managers.
★ Mistakes – How many do you make?
★ We all fear mistakes.
★ Our fear makes us hide mistakes.
★ Hence, our organisations hide mistakes, hence, unhappiness.

2

LEARN TO RE-THINK

Start Thinking

Mis-guided and inadequate thinking is the primary cause of just about all the world's ills.

It was a lack of rational thought that got Christians thrown to the lions in ancient Rome simply because they believed that God was not created by an Emperor's decree, that God was not manifest as a lump of carved rock, and that being nice to each other was quite a good idea.

It is fuzzy thinking which has led to the common industrial myth that *"Man is lazy and man is greedy, so we must combat his laziness by pampering to his greed."*

It is an example of intellectual crassness when we observe managers making operational decisions without reference to the free, expert advice from the workers actually doing the job.

It is mental sloppiness on a national scale when people talk of a Health Service (which demonstrably limits itself only to the management of illness) or an Employment Service (noted only for its work with the unemployed).

It is inadequate thinking that leads companies to pay salesmen bonuses based upon annual sales revenues. This drives them to sell what makes income in the short term, but which might not actually be profitable business and may not be what the customer actually needs. As a result of this the customer goes elsewhere for his next purchase, thereby killing the company in the long term.

The challenge is to think afresh – to think about your customers and your people differently. To think-through, develop and articulate an improved culture for your organisation. To think of the changes needed to the way you and your people approach work. To think about the business you are in and to question whether it really needs to become focused elsewhere. To think about your products and services, and to question whether they really meet the needs of the customers. To think about the relationships your organisation has with others, and whether what is said to your corporate face is the same as that said behind your collective back.

But be warned; this venture is not without risk. Thinking and challenging and questioning and making changes invariably put a strain on relationships within the organisation. Challenging accepted thinking takes supreme effort, inordinate patience and a very thick skin. That said, I have spent many fun-filled years "poking a stick" at the conventional wisdom of managers, clients and colleagues. I have found that as long as the "poking stick" has a padded end and that you wield it with sensitivity, the discomfort of yourself and others can be kept under control. Of course the real buzz comes when you encounter a kindred spirit.

They might be rare, but open-minded, free-thinking, creative, radical, results-oriented, action-focused managers do exist. They have a number of interesting characteristics in common.

They welcome outspoken ideas. They have the ability to use each idea and experience as a vehicle for learning about how they, and their organisation, can be improved. They are often popular with junior members of the organisation, being seen as a source of support, enthusiasm, ideas, and encouragement; or being used as a helpful sounding board, or being called upon to help remove a barrier to progress.

Their open-mindedness and love of ideas is, to many, the source of stimulation and encouragement, but is to others, a disturbing challenge or even a threat. They are despised by more blinkered peers who tender erroneous criticism about their ability or performance, frequently labelling them "mavericks" who are "a lot more trouble than they are worth." Those senior managers who have, over the years, become mentally rigid and stale often fear them. Invariably, very good at not showing their fear, these executives react to the "maverick" by setting him large-scale, high risk, high visibility goals, thereby "keeping him out of trouble" and providing a legitimate excuse to fire him if he fails. Paradoxically, this is often the most effective way to manage these so called "mavericks", as the very scale and challenge of the goal drives them to achieve their greatest successes.

Other characteristics of the free-thinking manager may deepen the perception that they are troublesome. They seldom attend internal meetings – generally having something better to do. They write few internal memos – preferring instead a quick phone call or, better, a face to face chat. They are always busy, but seldom look it, as they always have time to welcome a colleague who "has just popped in for a chat" about a problem or opportunity. Their routine monthly reports are frequently late and not very well produced, as they invest their time and efforts to ensuring that letters to customers or other important documents are produced on time and to the highest standards. They despise inter-departmental rivalry and politics, because they see the organisation as a whole. They appear to disregard completely the power structures of the organisation, talking freely to anyone who wants, or can provide, help. They make little effort to look good – being far too busy trying to be good.

The paradox often manifests itself at annual appraisal time; when the report carries fatuous pseudo-psychological criticisms of the manager's personality, but the objective assessment highlights some of the most significant contributions made to the business by anyone in the last year.

If you are such a manager, if you are convinced that there must a better way of running our institutions, if you do seek to make change, then this book and others like it are written for you. For it is you, and managers like you, who will extract the most value from them. The "closed-minded" will dismiss them. The "non-thinker" will perhaps enjoy the read but will learn little or nothing. The "passive learner" may gain new insight but will do nothing about it; and the "company smart-arse" (an all too common type of manager) will criticise this and similar books, dispute them, misquote them and abuse them, but will learn nothing and gain no benefit at all.

My hope is that the ideas, terminology, principles and implications surrounding continuous improvement, Customer Care, culture change and business excellence prove to be both entertaining and stimulating. In British organisations today, we need to think afresh. But in most of them, few of us think very much at all. It is only by re-thinking our businesses that we can secure the success we desire.

Tom Watson, the legendary head of IBM, understood this in the 1950s, when he coined, for every single employee in the largest and most powerful computer company in the world, the deceptively simple corporate motto: "THINK."

Only when we have re-thought, can we initiate change that is sustainable over the long haul. Our corporations and institutions are over-weight and out of condition. They will not survive the stress on their hearts that is caused by repeated crash diets, continued over indulgence and spasmodic bursts of high-energy exercise. They need a lifestyle change, which reduces the weight and sustains the standard of living. As with any lifestyle change, understanding and respecting the implications of the change requires very considerable thought.

As an aside, it is perhaps the unwillingness to invest sufficient effort in thought that has kept the diet industry so buoyant over the past three decades. If people would actually think through for themselves how they were going to change, not their eating habits but their lives, so as to balance food consumption with daily energy requirements, then the diet industry would cease to exist. Most of us (including me) are over-weight. And most of us at some time or other have tried to do something about it. We tried to diet. We ate fewer calories for as long as our enthusiasm held out. Then the low calorie recipe book was relegated to the back of the bookcase – until the next time. Those who got serious about it did something real and changed their entire lifestyle permanently. They could only have done that by thinking about it first. Perhaps thin people think best! Or perhaps they just think more about being thin.

The world of change management all starts with thinking differently. What should be different and hence what should change. The sixty-four thousand-dollar question is how do we learn to think differently?

Do we need to study Edward de Bono and the world of

lateral thinking? Well, yes that could be a very good idea. But then I would say that in response to *any* question of the form "should we study . . .?"

OK, would de Bono help us to think differently? Well, yes probably, but it would depend upon what you thought about what he said.

Oh this is silly! Is lateral thinking a tool to help us think differently or not? Well, yes for a lot of people on many occasions it is, but it does rather depend upon how you think now, what you are thinking about and how you actually go about thinking.

You see what I am saying is, that yes of course you should study the works of Edward de Bono. The man is obviously a genius and obviously has some wonderful ideas. But you should study everyone else you can get your hands on too – from Desmond Morris to Dilbert, from Sir John Harvey Jones to Douglas Adams. They all provide insights into different ways of thinking.

In Douglas Adams's book about space, time and the meaning of life, the universe and everything, *The Hitchhiker's Guide to the Galaxy*, every single page demonstrates new ways to think. From the mentally damaged "Marvin the paranoid android" who is always "very depressed" because the diodes down his left side hurt, to Adams's use of language when describing spacecraft over England as "the ships hung in the sky in much the same way as bricks don't."

Douglas Adams is not writing about business, nor is he writing about how managers should think. He is a creative genius writing a piece of escapist science fiction. However, when we open our minds, perhaps, just maybe, if the book tickled our cranial electrical bits enough, we find ourselves starting to ask different questions – "I wonder what would make Marvin especially depressed about our organisation?" or even possibly "I wonder what my organisation does 'like bricks don't'?"

The point is, that different stimuli affect different people, differently. So we all need to develop as open a mind as possible, which receives as much stimulation as possible, and we need to be as receptive as possible to the stimulation we receive, and also to recognise the effect such stimulants have upon our own thinking. This way, when we encounter a catalyst to thought that works for us – a particular author, a writing style, or whatever – we can seek more like it. It is axiomatic that "different folks need different strokes."

For me one of the most significant 'strokes' on business and management was *Up the Organisation* by Robert Townsend. This book had a profound effect upon the way I thought about management when, as a very junior team leader, I read it for the first time.

In common with any major learning experience, the divide between the ideas of the teacher and that of the student has become blurred. In my formative years in management, I became so attuned to the ideas expressed within his books, tapes and broadcasts, that now, years later, I cannot clearly separate in my mind which of my management beliefs and ideas are my own and which I have inherited from Mr Townsend. It must be twenty years since I looked at his book. Which ideas were lifted verbatim from him? Which of his ideas have I developed into my own? Which ideas are mine but were initiated by something unrelated that he wrote? Which ideas are completely mine and are in no way influenced by him at all? I cannot be certain.

Despite this, I do know that one idea, that I use all the time, definitely started with Bob Townsend.

It was from reading his books that I learned to manage

situations using "Opposite Thinking" [my title]. This is the idea that, for any situation, you should consider what the conventionally accepted management or institutional approach would be and then consider, very seriously, the diametric opposite. This one mental trick alone has proved to be more valuable to me than any other. Incidentally, the opposite of conventional wisdom is, in my experience, seldom worse, often as good and sometimes better than the more traditional approach.

As an exercise in opposite thinking, let us consider a very common aspect of conventional management wisdom that has been accepted as sensible for years – Management by Objectives. The following is an illustrative counter argument.

An Alternative Way of Thinking About Management by Objectives

"Organised Brain Death"

MBO is the most widely used system for managing people in the industrial world. The counter-argument runs, that even at its best, it not only does no good, it actually does positive harm to an organisation and the people within it. It creates conflict between those people that the organisation desperately needs to co-operate (a manager and his subordinate). It creates conflict in the one area of business where consensus is vital for commercial viability (planning deliverables). It positively drives under achievement from everyone in the organisation and, worst of all, prevents thinking.

So common is MBO that, inevitably, many of you (senior managers) will strongly disagree with this counter-argument and insist that I use a powerful justification to prove that I am not smoking pot. Rest assured, I do not

Rest assured, I do not use "funny" cigarettes.

use "funny" cigarettes (or any other illegal substances come to that) and a justification will be forthcoming.

So obvious is the down-side of MBO that, inevitably, many of you (typically lower down the organisation pyramid) will be nodding vigorously while at the same time pleading "But how do we kill it off? It's in the company woodwork!" Sadly, this is not easy unless you are the Chief Executive when all that is needed is for you to yell very loudly at your next board meeting. Sacred cows are tough beasts and take some killing; the lower down the heap you are the harder it is. Take heart, it can be done with guerrilla tactics, but it takes time.

So, how can I claim that MBO is to business organisations what King Herod was to baby-sitting?

Well, let's think. To help us think we will use a couple of

mental techniques. The first of these is "The Safe Mental Environment". This means creating in our mind a fictitious but intellectually viable environment in which a particular scenario can be played out to its logical conclusion. The second technique needs no explanation as we've all used it as children (though many of us have now forgotten how); it is called "Let's Pretend".

Our "Safe Mental Environment" is Vertical Risers Plc, a well-managed and reasonably successful company that uses MBO. This company is in the "going-up" business. In other words, the higher its people rise, the better. We are silent and invisible observers who are blessed with limited powers of clairvoyance and a useful ability to be in two places at the same time. Now, we can pretend.

It is 09:00 on Monday morning and worker Bill is preparing for his annual objectives setting meeting at 10:00 with his boss John. Bill knows his job – going up, but how high? That's the question. His annual objective will be a target height from the ground. He also knows that Vertical Risers Plc operates a "Pay For Performance" policy. Managers and staff who meet their objectives can expect a reasonable annual pay increase, and those who exceed them will get bigger rises and possibly even promotion. Bill muses that there aren't many who fail to achieve their objectives – they don't stay with the company too long. Bill starts to feel uncomfortable, he really does need to turn in a good performance this year, last year's achievements were OK . . . but only OK, another mediocre year and questions will be asked about his soundness. Bill thinks hard.

"Now, I'm six foot tall, if I stand on my desk and jump that's ten feet. If I put a chair on my desk that's about twelve feet. No, this is hopeless, I've got to do better than that. Oh! Just a minute, if I stand on the roof of the office block, that's 200 feet, yes that's better. So if I find a really big tower block I might get to 600 feet. OK, now I'm ready for my meeting with John."

At the same time John is preparing for his objectives meetings with Bill and he goes through a similar thought process. Coincidentally, he arrives at a figure of 600 feet too.

At this point, let us look into the minds of Bill and John. Bill thinks that if he can get his objective set lower than 600 feet he can exceed it and improve his reputation. He also recognises the need to build in a safety margin because to fail (even by a tiny amount) would be a disaster. Bill settles on a negotiating position of 500 feet. John, on the other hand, thinks that by setting a demanding objective he will motivate Bill to work hard. So he sets his negotiating position at 700 feet.

The meeting takes place. John gives his usual speech about difficult trading conditions, increased competition and the need for everyone to pull their weight and says how much he values Bill as someone who is willing to accept demanding targets and work so hard – the sort of person that Vertical Risers needs. Bill gives his usual speech about being a reliable, good company man who is always ready for a challenge, but noting how the environment in which he works does limit his overall potential. Clichés over, they get down to the serious business of holding the auction. They finally settle on, yes you've guessed it, 600 feet.

So what's wrong with that?

What's right with it!

The combined thinking time spent setting the objective was two hours. Two hours thought for a year's work. That has got to be wrong. Throughout the encounter Bill and John were in the conflict of a negotiation. No wonder quality guru Philip B Crosby, and others, have noted that "Management can be a curse from God, whereas they should be there to help you." The target actually ended up being very, very soft. And worst of all there is a good chance that Bill will fail.

Let's play in our Safe Mental Environment a little longer.

Bill knows he can stand on a building for 600 feet. With a trivial amount of further thought he realises that taking a desk and chair up to the roof he could achieve 612 feet. He also recognises that as long as he exceeds 600 feet he will be OK. It is day one of the year and already his objective is in the bag. With no challenge, Bill coasts. He has to look busy. Everyone in every company has to do that, all the time (More evidence, if it were needed, of a lack of thought in our institutions.) So, he attends meetings. These serve no real purpose for him, but he feels obliged to make some contribution. Of course, this means that he interferes with the work of everyone else. The upshot of all this is that he doesn't actually get round to trying to achieve his objective until the end of the year. Unfortunately, when Bill does get around to doing something, he discovers that the company has imposed a travel ban in order to protect cash flow, so he is prevented from going to find the tall building. He panics and forgets that he could stand on his own office block (for 200 feet) and jumps onto his desk achieving a pitiful 12 feet.

Staying within our Safe Mental Environment we can now postulate alternatives.

There is an alternative to MBO. In my counter-argument, we can call it GBO (The Glaringly Bloody Obvious) or we might call it MBV – Management By Vision.

Bill and John know the vision that "up is good, higher is better". Both Bill and John have the same mission – to get Bill up. There is no such thing as failure only degrees of success. In this Safe Mental Environment we could play Let's Pretend again to think about their first meeting of the year. It would be more like this. "Well, how high do you think you could get Bill?"

"I reckon if I found a big building I could make 600 feet what do you think?"

"That's better than my idea. My best thought was that if you stood on a chair on the top of your desk and jumped you could get 12 feet."

"But hang on, that idea is good, we can add them together making 612 feet."

"OK, you go and do that while I try to think about something even better."

A week later our heroes meet again. Bill has achieved his 612 feet in the first week of the year and John has had a further few hours to think. "Well done Bill, now I've been thinking. What about the top of a mountain that could give us thousands of feet? Everest is how big? 26,000?"

"I think it's more like 29,000 feet, but it would take me forever to learn to be a good enough mountaineer to climb it carrying my desk."

"You're right of course Bill. We'd better set our sights lower. What about one of the Alps? You can get a cable car to the top."

"I'm not giving up that easily. I've been thinking too. Look, airliners cruise above the mountains, Concorde flies way above, I'm not sure how high, but it must give us 50,000 feet. There's a flight to the West Indies in a couple of hours, I think I should be on it. Oh, and by the way, England are being put in to bat tomorrow, may I have a

I doubt if I could climb it carrying my desk.

couple of days leave before I come back?"

OK, so it was only pretend. OK it was simplistic. But a different way of thinking got Bill to achieve significantly more than 50,000 feet in less than two weeks, as opposed to failing to achieving a pitiful 12 feet in a year – makes ya think dunnit!

Somebody Else's Problem

A little while ago I was having a quiet beer and a chat with the Managing Director of an engineering company. (I'll call him John.) The conversation was friendly and relaxed, until I brought the subject round to quality. At this point he became more intense. "Oh don't start on that again," he said. "Look, my organisation is bright, and go-ahead. We employ great people, and we've got a good management team. It's a well-run outfit. Our customers like the product and we have a well-deserved reputation for quality. We regularly innovate and bring ever better products to market. Our people are generally happy at work and generally do a good job. The business is doing well and our profits are healthy. We take quality very seriously – everyone knows how important it is.

"Of course things do occasionally go wrong. Customers do occasionally complain. We even lose a few customers to the competition, but life's like that. We win more new customers than we lose, so we are obviously getting it right.

"Mind you, I know of lots of companies that do need to get their act together with quality. Firms are going bust all the time. Even some of our suppliers need to re-think it. Only last week we had to return a batch of mouldings because a bunch of cowboys had supplied the wrong size."

I asked John how he discovered this fault. He obviously thought my question stupid as he replied, "Because the thing wouldn't fit when we tried to assemble it of course!"

"So what did you do then?" I asked.

"It was a nightmare! The customer was on the phone all the time nagging us about delivery dates and threatening us with blue murder if we didn't deliver on time. By Tuesday, I wasn't doing any real work at all; I spent the whole day on the phone, either talking to the customer's MD trying to keep him sweet or to the supplier's MD to lay it on the line to him. To his credit, he pulled out all the stops and got the correct parts to us by Thursday. They weren't the colour we asked for, but that wasn't a major problem. All we needed to do was give them a re-spray before we built the product. We delivered the consignment to the customer only one day behind schedule and he seemed pleased that we were able to sort things out."

I have conversations like this with managers regularly. Some are in the manufacturing business, some are in research, some are in the service sector and others are in government. With the vast majority of them the message is the same and boils down to:

We are doing OK . . . *so don't need to change.*
We take it seriously now . . . *so don't need to change.*
Of course, other companies need to change . . . *but not us.*
Things go wrong ("their" fault) but we fix it . . . *so don't need to change.*

My conversation with John continued and I gently suggested to him that perhaps he really did have "just a few" (sic) quality problems. We talked about his existing market and his potential market and about his existing competitors and his potential competitors. Unsurprisingly, topics such as time to market, speed of innovation, margin erosion, failure costs, hidden failure costs, etc., were discussed. Slowly, he started to see for himself that perhaps it wasn't somebody else's problem after all.

"So what we're saying is that suppliers really are my problem. If they get it wrong, I cannot get it right. Re-spraying those sub-components cost me money. The days we spent waiting for the right parts were, at best, spent inefficiently – costing me more money. The customer seemed happy with what we did, but not happy enough to be willing to be a reference for us. And do you know what . . ." he looked sheepish ". . . If I'm brutally frank with you, I've just realised that the reason the supplier got it wrong in the first place was because he thought we specified the part in centimetres, while we thought we had specified inches. But nobody confirmed the order in writing. So the real root cause could possibly all have been our fault. Mmm! I'll have to have a serious chat with my buyer when I get back into the office."

"Yes," I said, "It certainly sounds as if the buyer's procedures . . ."

". . . Oh God! I see where you're going. As Managing Director it is my job to set down the policies, under which everyone in the company operates, and it is from these policies that all the procedures and regulations in the company follow. So if a procedure is inadequate it is either because my policy was inadequate or it is because I have an inadequate policy for policing procedures. So I suppose that it was all ultimately *my* fault, or at the very least, it was down to me to have prevented the problem from arising – oh hell!"

John was now thinking clearly and had reached a vital stage. By recognising the possibility that it *could* have been his fault, he was starting to develop an open mind. And, lest we forget, an open mind allows the truth in, while a closed mind keeps it out.

John was also beginning to see his personal accountability in a different light. He may, or may not, have been the cause of the problem. But irrespective of whose fault it actually was, he was personally accountable to his customer. John's company had promised to deliver a product to the customer and had failed to do so.

In other words, John's company, and by implication John himself, had lied.

As far as the customer is concerned, everyone in John's company with whom he has contact *is* the company.

Therefore, everyone in the company had lied to him (knowingly or otherwise). Truth and honesty are personal values and therefore the accountability for them must rest with individuals. Of course with John himself as MD all of this goes double – "He carries the can – The buck stops here."

So, the more accountable an individual becomes, the more authority s/he has. And obviously, with authority comes responsibility. As we shall see later, the implications of this remark have a considerable impact upon an organisation's strategies.

John's example is nothing out of the ordinary. Companies have quality problems; hospitals have them, so do schools, clubs and societies. And so do individuals.

Another Day's Mistakes
As you know from Chapter 1, one of my favourite little exercises is to ask people how many mistakes they make personally in the average day.

This exercise is actually more effective when I use it within a classroom setting to a group of people, as this enables me to pick on one poor unsuspecting individual and insist on a precise numeric answer. Eventually, after much squirming and many excuses, my first victim will reply with a number (usually about ten). I then pick on someone else and ask again. This time there is less discomfort ("Well, he didn't kill him, so it's probably OK for me to own-up too"), and my second victim replies with a number – usually the same, or very similar, to the first's. I then ask a third person who usually replies confidently with, often, a much bigger number than the first two. We then have a short discussion on the psychology of why the third person was so confident while the first was so unsure, and from this we draw conclusions about fear of mistakes in our organisations.

I then tell the group that this question was *not* the important one.

The important question is *how many mistakes do you* **want to make** *in the average day*? Naturally, my three victims this time all confidently answer "none at all."

This exercise works at a number of different levels. It shows the group that quality failures are the responsibility of the individual (mistakes made by you personally) and it shows that this responsibility must be focused before improvement can occur (how many mistakes specifically, precisely?). It demonstrates that everyone naturally wants to do well (how many mistakes do you *want to make*?) and implies that everyone is willing to improve (we all make mistakes, but not by design).

The exercise also shows the group how important it is to create an environment where mistakes can be admitted. Without the admission that mistakes exist, no investigation and no improvement will be made.

Each member of the group discovers for him/herself that fears of reprisal are a significant inhibitor to the admission of mistakes. It shows that once the fear has been removed, the recognition of failure becomes a positive motivator for improvement.

Now it is your turn again. Following you will find a Personal Checklist. Place a tick in any box where you can honestly answer the question "Yes". Any box, which yields a "No" answer, is an indication of an endemic quality problem in your organisation, which will affect your local team's, and your own performance.

A PERSONAL CHECKLIST

☐ Do you have a clear and agreed job description, stating both your responsibilities and authority?

☐ Do you understand the purpose of the task that your work-group performs in the organisation?

☐ Do you know the critical success factors of your work-group and how they are measured?

☐ Do you have personal critical success factors and do you measure them?

☐ Do you know the critical success factors of your manager and his work-group and how these are measured?

☐ Do you know what is expected of you regarding the quality of your work?

☐ Do you measure what proportion of your time is spent on re-work or correcting your own or other people's mistakes?

☐ Do you measure what it costs in terms of time and effort to put things right when they go wrong?

☐ Is your work and the work of your team always completed satisfactorily and on time?

☐ Do you have easy access to everything that you need to do your job?

Score out of 10 = ...

Let's just take a look at that checklist again and ask, "What is behind the questions?"

Do you have a clear and agreed job description, stating both your responsibilities and authority? If not, how do you know what your job is? If you don't know what your job is, how can you judge if you are doing it right? Why haven't you found out?

Do you understand the purpose of the task that your work-group performs in the organisation? If not, how do you make judgments about the validity of any decisions you make?

Do you know the critical success factors of your work-group and how they are measured? If not, how can you tell if you are meeting the needs of the business?

Do you have personal critical success factors and do you measure them? If not, how do you know how your performance, and hence your rewards, are to be judged and how do you set an agenda for your subordinates that supports you?

Do you know the critical success factors of your manager and his work-group and how these are measured? If not, how can you best help him? And if you don't help him, why should he help you?

Do you know what is expected of you regarding the quality of your work? If not, how can you have confidence that you are really meeting the needs of the customer?

Do you measure what proportion of your time is spent on re-work or correcting your own or other people's mistakes? If not, how do you judge the impact of mistakes? How can you evaluate which mistakes are important and must be sorted out now, and which are minor and can be dealt with when you have more time?

Do you measure what it costs in terms of time and effort to put things right when they go wrong? If not, how do you judge whether you are operating competitively – both as an individual and as an organisation?

Is your work and the work of your team always completed satisfactorily and on time? If not, you know you have problems? Where does the buck stop?

Do you have easy access to everything that you need to do your job? If not, you are failing to manage your organisation in such a way as to help you to make an optimum contribution to the business. You are allowing the organisation to help you to fail.

In a five-year period, between 1987 and 1992, I conducted this test with more than 1,000 directors, managers and staff from small, medium and large companies. No one scored more than 8 and most scored 3, 4 or 5!

There isn't a single company that's good enough. There isn't a single business leader or manager who doesn't screw-up. This is not somebody else's problem. In organisations today, we simply don't have the time or the resources to fear and hide our mistakes. If we don't admit them, we won't address them. If we don't address them, the competition will wipe us out.

What is Quality?
So, given that we need to do something about quality, we had better start by defining what we mean by the term quality itself.

In fact, I am not going to give you a definition at all. Instead, I will discuss a number of them. The reason for this is that in your organisation you are trying to create a common view about quality and an approach to improvement that uses the skills, energies and enthusiasm of everyone in the organisation. You therefore need to define quality in your organisation clearly and communicate it. You also need to convince everyone of the value of your definition. If I gave you one definition only, it would be mine not yours and you would never be able to communicate it as effectively as you would your own.

The first place to look for a definition of a word is a dictionary, so let's start there. *The Little Oxford Dictionary* defines quality as: "Degree of excellence, attribute; relative nature or kind or character; timbre." Other dictionaries provide variations on this theme. But in summary, quality, according to the English dictionaries, means degree of excellence or goodness.

This is a very useful definition if you are the customer. As customers, we assess the quality of a product against our own views of excellence and goodness. We decide what is and what is not quality and we do it judgmentally and in our own individual terms. And we do it so often and so naturally that we are frequently unaware that we are doing so. You have only got to listen to a few guys talking about cars to see what I mean.

"Well . . . err . . . I have been very pleased with my Skoda."

"Now, that BMW is a real quality car!"

"Yeah it's OK but it's not as good as the Ferrari."

"You know speed isn't everything. If you want quality, look at the Rolls Royce."

"Well . . .err . . . I've been very pleased with my Skoda."

"Skoda!!? Quality . . . don't make me laugh!"

"Well, it does hold the world record for having more class victories in international rallies than any other car. It has won its class in the British RAC rally 26 times in the last 27 years. I've had mine for seven years and it's never gone wrong and it's cheap to run and fun to drive."

"Oh . . . I see . . . Nah! I still like the BMW."

Which one of them is right? Which is the quality car – BMW, Ferrari, Rolls Royce or Skoda? With the dictionary definition, we cannot tell. All we can do is argue about it. The dictionary definition is fine if you are the customer sitting in judgment, but is no use if you are trying to gain a common view of quality throughout an organisation and is no help to you in predicting how your customers will judge you and your products.

There are many other definitions of quality that have been developed over the years by gurus in the field. I will summarise three of the most well known.

Philip B Crosby defined it as: "Conformance to requirements." W Edwards Deming said: "Quality is continually meeting customers' needs and expectations at a price that they are willing to pay." While Joseph M Juran defined quality as: "Fitness for intended use."

These definitions, while differing, are not wildly at variance. Though you might not think so if you heard these men talking. At first glance, they seem very different in style and concept. For example, "Needs and expectations" appears to be more attitudes oriented than "requirements", only one definition includes "price", while only one has the concept of the end user. Actually, they are all saying much the same thing. A "requirement" is only a "requirement" once it has been agreed to be so between a customer and a supplier. This simply cannot be achieved without there being a relationship between the two of them, and such a relationship must be based upon needs, expectations, price and the end-use to which the product or service being proposed will be put.

The point, which is common to these definitions, including the dictionary definition, is this: the customer, not the supplier, ultimately assesses quality. The gurus' definitions score over the dictionary's definition, because they are phrased in such a way as to allow you to invest in making them happen.

The question, which is fundamental to these definitions, is what does the customer demand, want and expect? This implies that, as the supplier, you know who the customer is, and what his needs are. It also implies that you translate these needs into terms that are meaningful in your operation.

The International Standards Organisation (ISO) has also defined quality, as: "The totality of features and characteristics of a product or service that bears on its ability to satisfy stated or implied needs." This definition is perhaps the clearest of them all. It is a definition that needs little explanation and is considered by many companies to be the best definition. There is one possible problem with it though. It is perhaps somewhat long and dull. If you can't remember it and it doesn't excite you, action is unlikely to follow.

So, there are many different ways to express quality, but at the fundamental level these differing views have much in common.

Customers buy that which is of value to them. If the perceived value is higher than the perceived cost, then the customer will perceive quality; if it isn't, he won't.

What you must do is decide how quality will be defined in your organisation. Any of the definitions summarised here can be made to work for you. The vital thing is to get a definition and stick to it. Once you have a definition with which you are completely comfortable, tell everyone, explain it to everyone, explain the implications of it to everyone, and explain to everyone what they must now start to do.

LEARN TO RE-THINK
A Summary For Browsers

Start Thinking
* ★ Think afresh.
* ★ But this is not easy.
* ★ All input can help you think differently.
* ★ The opposite of conventional wisdom.
* ★ The Safe Mental Environment.
* ★ Let's Pretend.

Illustrative Counter Example
* ★ A counter-argument – Management by Objectives sucks!

Somebody Else's Problem
* ★ Many organisations think they take quality seriously.
* ★ Few actually do.
* ★ Few recognise their own mistakes and problems, preferring to blame someone else.
* ★ Not just businesses have quality problems. Schools, clubs, churches, etc., do too.
* ★ Individuals have them too.

Another Day's Mistakes
* ★ The Fear Factor revisited.
* ★ A personal checklist.

What is Quality?

★ "Degree of excellence, attribute; relative nature or kind or character; timbre."

★ "Conformance to requirements."

★ "Quality is continually meeting customers' needs and expectations at a price that they are willing to pay."

★ "Fitness for intended use."

★ "The totality of features and characteristics of a product or service that bears on its ability to satisfy stated or implied needs."

★ "Customers buy that which is of value to them. If the perceived value is higher than the perceived cost, then the customer will perceive quality; if it isn't, he won't.

★ Make one definition your own.

3

CHANGE THROUGH PROCESS MANAGEMENT

The World of Change

Ensuring that you deliver value does not happen by accident. It must be planned. Your approach must ensure that the right things are designed and developed. These must then be made correctly, at an acceptable cost and sold at an acceptable profit. Furthermore, your approach needs to ensure that all this is done consistently.

As customers become more demanding so the need for improvement becomes more apparent. With the increase in competition globally, the need for action becomes ever more urgent. So, it becomes glaringly obvious that we must monitor and investigate our customers and competitors at a level previously unprecedented. In the days of Henry Ford, you could have any colour you liked as long as it was black. Today you can buy a Range Rover in literally any colour you like. Why? Because BMW offer the same service, as do other car makers. If Henry Ford operated to his 'only black' principles today, he'd probably go bust (or he'd win a cult following from such an eccentric marketing stunt).

Be in no doubt, the need for urgent action to make real improvements to the way in which we operate our

He'd win a cult following from such an eccentric marketing stunt.

organisations is staring us all in the face. Take the UK as an example. Britain used to have a reputation for providing the best education in the world. Sadly, it no longer holds this position. Britain used to have the finest health service in the world. Tragically, for the nation's sick, this is no longer the case. Britain used to have one of, if not the, highest standard of living in the world. Frustratingly, for all of us here, it has it no longer. Britain used to be internationally recognised and respected as a super-power. The British used to be admired the world over for exemplary good manners and standards of behaviour. It used to be the case that the British lived according to "family values"; today it is an empty political sound bite. In Britain, churches are emptying, while crime is on the increase, and the number of crimes against people is increasing even faster. Job security is lower in Britain than in many of her competitor countries, earnings per employee are lower too, while costs are higher. The list goes on and on.

Absolutely every organisation in the land, large or small, business or social, must take action to improve. Even where we are the best, history tells us that we will fail to sustain that position if we stand still. In the organisations which continue to compete and continue to enjoy a good reputation, the message that the successful have learned, and taken to their hearts, is:

"We might be succeeding, but for how long? We cannot ever be complacent. We must always keep our eyes and ears open."

The less successful haven't even realised that there is a threat out there. They sit in their air-conditioned offices with the doors and windows tightly closed, blissfully unaware that their customers want something else and their competitors are developing ways of providing it. Then, later, there is no air-conditioned office, the boards go up, and no one really understands why – until the next time.

The successful know that change is everywhere and they have known it from the time of the ancient Greeks, when the philosopher Heraclitis observed, "There is nothing permanent except change."

In recent decades, perhaps the best example has been in the computer industry.

In the ten years 1982-1992 some of the changes demanded by computer customers were awesome. For instance, in 1982 the largest general-purpose data processing mainframe computer could support around 300 users, by 1992 this figure had risen to well over 8,000.

In 1982 mainframe computers typically crashed several times in a week, and the customers didn't expect anything better. By 1992 end-user expectation was that mainframes never failed. In reality the systems crashed about once per year, but even this represents an improvement of between 50,000% and 100,000%.

One year later, by 1993, it was the widely accepted wisdom of industry pundits that the mainframe computer was a fundamentally redundant technology and that sales of such systems would be zero within five years. Personally, I did not believe these predictions, but they were right to the extent that the development of the PC certainly made a large number of mainframe applications obsolete and will no doubt continue to do so. In the 1980s the mainframe was the only viable business computer, by the 1990s it had been replaced as a general-purpose technology by the PC and Network Server. Today, the mainframe is being used for what it is best at – the storage and simple manipulation of truly vast quantities of data. Increasingly, organisations are recognising the economic advantage of using the mainframe to bulk-store data centrally and to use distributed PCs to perform rapid complex manipulations of small data packets. Computer technology today is becoming integrated. For how long this will continue to be the case is still a matter of some debate in the industry.

The development of the PC itself shows a simply astonishing rate of change. Not just the technology and the software, but the effect it is having upon our everyday lives. Ten years ago, PCs generally didn't work, had insufficient power, were unreliable and were only used by specialists and enthusiasts. Today, virtually every kid in the country is, to some extent, PC literate. Five years ago, I regularly heard senior managers say something like, "Oh I don't understand those things, I leave all that to the computer department." Today, I cannot recall a single senior manager who doesn't have ready access to computer technology and who doesn't know how to use it.

In just fifteen years, talking to computers has developed from typing unintelligible computer codes onto punched cards, to typing text onto green screens, to moving icons around coloured screens, to the intuitive manipulation of pictures, sounds, and video around automated stereo multi-media systems.

In less than a decade, computer technology has created, quite literally, a Cultural Revolution which will affect us all. The development of the Internet and World-wide Web has created a global "common language" for communications and information processing. Today it is entirely feasible to imagine a five-year-old sitting playing on her dad's PC in Russia, sharing a picture she had drawn with another child in Beijing, who, in turn, adds his own bits to the picture and passes it to his pen-pal in the States. The whole process could literally be performed in minutes and each child would understand what each other child was doing – despite the three different native languages and cultures, and a complete absence of any formal computer training for any of them.

"Information Globalisation" is here now and is an issue, and opportunity, of quite spectacular proportions. Its potential is to change not just information flow but the entire culture of the planet and, perhaps most significantly of all, the way that everyone in the world actually thinks.

As for the industry itself over the last decade, it has seen many losers and some winners. The winners know absolutely about the need for change. They know absolutely that change is driven by customer demand. They know absolutely that if they fail to meet these demands they will die. They know absolutely that somewhere in the world someone else is producing something better than they can offer.

It isn't just in the computer industry where the winners know these things. Winners in every sector know them – even the most traditional.

Rugby football is an English traditional game, started in the public schools, which for years has been played in the same time honoured fashion. *"Rugger"* is a small part of Britain's national heritage.

Unfortunately, the foreign competition in the Southern Hemisphere didn't think much of public schoolboy tradition. The game was never going to be *"Rugger"* to them. The South Africans, New Zealanders, Australians and Fijians started, *"in a most ungentlemanly and unseemly fashion,"* to play the game to win. The New Zealand All Blacks started it, by developing a "corporate strategy" which had as its overall aim the elimination of all errors from the field of play. Southern clubs started to pay players a salary and insist upon standards of performance that they measured objectively. They invested in stadiums and facilities for spectators that secured the money needed for the development of the game. They did deals with the media. They re-designed international competition, and ultimately re-engineered the game itself.

In England, while this was going on, our clubs were singing Eskimo Nell and drinking heavily. Despite some occasional spectacular performances by British players, it became very clear that British rugby had to change or die.

The winners know that change is driven by competition, but they know that it is driven most by customer demand.

Customers constantly demand more; and this isn't just the case in the high-tech world. All businesses are subject to customer pressure to change and improve. The family car in the 1970s typically started to rust after a couple of years; today 6-10 year anti-corrosion warranties are the norm. You probably used to rent your TV, because then someone else would maintain it. Today, you probably own your set – it doesn't go wrong. Not so long ago, you

Singing Eskimo Nell.

would boil and bleach your whites; today you use a low temperature automatic washing powder. If you like foreign food, you used to go to very highly-priced restaurants to get it; today your local supermarket will sell you a complete pre-prepared banquet from the country of your choice for little more (if any) than the price you would pay for more traditional fare.

Customers constantly demand more; and this isn't just the case with products, it applies equally as much to services. More of us buy more services now than ever before. For example, having a personal bank account is common place today – it used not to be.

When we use these services, we become more demanding. We want better. For instance, banks have now extended their services to pay your bills for you by Standing Order, and many major organisations seek your agreement to gain direct access to your bank account so that they can take any payment due via Direct Debit. Telephone banking is becoming more widespread, so that you can avail yourself of the bank's services without the inconvenience of leaving your home. Automated banking has now been launched, enabling you to use your home computer to manage your finances for you and communicate directly to your bank's computers for implementation.

Not only do customers constantly demand more and demand better, they also demand cheaper. Customers constantly demand better value for money. We all are aware of inflation, and know that things used to be cheaper than they are today. However, in real terms, many things cost less today than they did. When I was eight I had a shilling (5p) per week pocket money. My eight-year-old son has a pound per week (an increase of 20 times!). When I was eight a bar of chocolate cost sixpence (2.5p) – half of my weekly income; today the same bar would cost about 30p – a third of my son's income.

As we become more demanding, so we demand more for less. No longer is it acceptable for us to pay bank charges for the dubious privilege of having a chequebook that enables the bank to have free use of our money. Today most banks actually pay us interest on our current accounts. Similarly, a number of major organisations now offer a discount to those customers who agree to pay bills via Direct Debit. We enjoy a more convenient way to pay and they pay us for the privilege.

The challenge that faces your organisation is the customer demand for more, better, cheaper. To enable you to satisfy this insatiable demand for more, better, cheaper, your organisation must change and change constantly. To change, it must learn, plan, and control what it does. It must reduce its cost base constantly, and it must innovate like crazy. For this to be profitable it must do all of this with quality in mind at every stage.

To do all of this with quality in mind at all stages, you must have a plan, you must invest in control systems, and you must invest in systems that solve problems once and for all. You must educate and train your people. You must give your people the freedom and the environment to try new things out. In essence, you need a systematic approach with unprecedented levels of monitoring and control and you need, paradoxically, to give your people unprecedented freedom and authority.

How Do You Deliver Value?

As with the definition of the word "quality", many experts have attempted to prescribe how to make quality happen in an organisation. For example Joseph M Juran has explained it this way:

"Quality should be managed in the same way as any other business function. Within the Finance function, there are three key processes involved:

— Budgeting
— Cost/Expenditure control
— Cost reduction/profit improvement.

Budgeting is just a specialised form of planning. Expenditure control involves monitoring and regulation. Cost reduction is about driving improvements. The 'Trilogy' for quality is essentially just the same:

— Quality Planning
— Quality Control
— Quality Improvement."

He went on to talk of planning by saying that: "A lack of Quality Planning has been, and continues to be, the biggest single contributory cause of the quality crisis of recent years." He claimed that this led to a chronic cost of poor quality: "About a third of all work in the US economy consists of redoing things previously done wrong," he said. "This situation has prevailed in the USA for so long that it is almost endemic and can only be addressed by direct upper management intervention."

Juran believed that management controllable defects accounted for 85% of the totality of quality problems, the remaining 15% being attributable to "Special causes" (e.g. raw material faults, mis-handling, worker error, etc.).

In contrast to these views, W Edwards Deming said: "People work IN a system, while managers work ON a system." In other words, managers create processes while workers operate processes. Management controllable errors, according to both men, are those errors that are built into the process by managers. However, Deming asserted that the scale of management controllable errors is even greater. In his opinion the ratio is nearer to 94% to 6%.

Philip Crosby has made a similar set of points. He too talked of companies' failure costs, which he called "The Price Of Non-Conformance". He estimated that in manufacturing companies the equivalent of 40% of sales was spent annually in re-work, error correction and other failure activities. He went on to say that in the service sector this figure was even higher. The issue of management commitment to quality improvement was fundamental to Crosby's approach to quality management. He didn't talk of planning, control and improvement in the same way as Juran, but he did advocate that management is held accountable for its influence on quality (or lack of it). He made the unequivocal assertion that companies must learn to *prevent* problems, not fix them after they have happened. "Learn to do it right the first time," he said. While Crosby did not make planning and control the explicit thrust of his argument, preferring instead to champion "prevention" as the way to achieve quality, it is self evident that prevention would be impossible without a planned and controlled approach. Crosby's "Do it right first time" was his link between prevention and management commitment. To "do it right first time" you must prevent failures and you must set a standard to everyone in the organisation, which states that errors are unacceptable. Crosby called this standard "Zero Defects". Zero Defects is the management attitude to business, which drives everyone in the organisation.

Again, the "gurus" have expressed themselves in different ways, but again there are common themes.

You will only deliver value to your customers if managers ensure that the processes that create the products or services are correctly designed, developed, operated and controlled.

So, a key to managing improvement is managing processes. But what is a process?

A process is a series of actions or events which causes something to happen or be provided – a desired outcome. Processes can take many forms. A process may be made up of any number of activities or sub-processes which combine (serially, or in parallel, or any combination of both) to provide outputs. The recipients of these outputs may be known as "customers" of the process – whether they are customers of the organisation or not. In this way, customer/supplier relationships may be developed both inside and outside the business.

If a process is correctly designed, developed, operated and controlled, then it will produce correct output, which can be monitored. If the recipient of a process's output is a customer, then this monitoring can be made against customer requirements.

If a process fails to meet customer requirements, or an opportunity for improvement is identified, then the process can be changed.

The thing to recognise from all of this is that you can actually do something positive. You can start to think seriously about your customers and what they want. You can start to recognise that every single output from your business comes from a process. You can investigate these processes to ensure that they do what you think they do and they are controlled so that they do them consistently. You can recognise that there are internal processes in your organisation whose outputs are the inputs to the next processes in the value chain. You can invest time and effort to understand this value chain better, what it costs, what it yields, how it works, who it satisfies, who it dissatisfies. In short, you can start Process Management.

However, before we get there, it might be helpful to put a little structure around these ideas. With all this talk of definitions of quality, quality trilogies, zero defects and so on, it becomes easy to give up in a puff of jargon. So how do you attain quality?

Let's look at the parameters.

First, we need something that will make improvements happen. Improvements can only happen if we either put some fault right so that it never happens again, or if we make some process improvement. For example, redesign some process to make it better, or streamline a process to make it more efficient, or reduce a process to make it simpler.

Next, we need to consider improving everything. To

mis-quote Sir Isaac Newton, "For every action there is a reaction," and to not mis-quote John Donne, "No man is an island." In other words, everything that is done in an organisation affects something, and someone, else. If we are seriously considering improving everything, we must recognise that this is going to be hard and is going take a while.

In fact, by the time we've managed to get through everything, the environment will have changed so much that we will have to start again – decorating the house to meet the desires of a wife and two teenagers springs instantly to mind!

We need therefore to establish a system for continuous improvement – one that runs forever; and that means that it must be cyclic.

If the improvements we make apply to processes, we must measure and monitor these to help us understand how they are working, and we must make real decisions based upon the measurements we make.

Finally, if we are going to make improvements by modifying processes, we must plan our actions scientifically to ensure that we take the right actions, for the right reasons and that they have the right effects.

These are our basic parameters for making quality happen. It is now a relatively simple Systems Analysis and Design task to create a high-level systems model to meet these parameters and hence establish a structure for quality improvement and continuous improvement. A sample design is shown in figure 1.

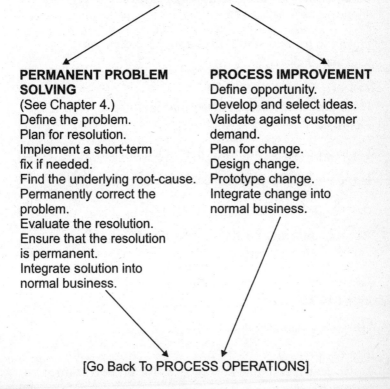

NEW PROCESS PLANNING
Identify customers.
Define customer needs, wants and expectations.
Design process to meet customer demand.
Prototype process to prove correct functionality.

PROCESS OPERATIONS
Run the process.
Measure and monitor process operations for the purpose
of process control.
Measure and monitor process for the purpose of evaluation.

**PERMANENT PROBLEM
SOLVING**
(See Chapter 4.)
Define the problem.
Plan for resolution.
Implement a short-term
fix if needed.
Find the underlying root-cause.
Permanently correct the
problem.
Evaluate the resolution.
Ensure that the resolution
is permanent.
Integrate solution into
normal business.

PROCESS IMPROVEMENT
Define opportunity.
Develop and select ideas.
Validate against customer
demand.
Plan for change.
Design change.
Prototype change.
Integrate change into
normal business.

[Go Back To PROCESS OPERATIONS]

Fig. 1. An example systems model.

The Process Rule-base

The following questions may be considered throughout the life cycle of any process. You should add other questions to this checklist, which you find valuable.

Process Planning:

Are requirements for the process outputs formally agreed with customers? ☐

Is there a mission covering this process? ☐

Are the process objectives clearly stated? (I.e. are they Specific, Measurable, Achievable, Relevant, and Time-based [SMART]?) ☐

Have the process standards and tolerances been articulated clearly? ☐

Process Engineering:

Have process owner, designer and user been identified? ☐

Is the process development plan documented? ☐

Is there a helpful review mechanism in place? ☐

Are the process sub-elements defined? ☐

Are requirements for the process inputs formally agreed with suppliers? ☐

Are the interfaces to other processes defined and understood? ☐

Have all assumptions been risk-assessed? ☐

Process Control:

Have clear measurement standards for process control been defined? ☐

Has a way of regulating performance been developed? ☐

Process Improvement:

Have process weak points and stress points been identified in advance? ☐

Do you know how the process will be proven? ☐

Do you know how the process will be piloted? ☐

Has the process been fully documented? ☐

Is there a communicated and agreed introduction plan for the process? ☐

Is everyone who is or could be affected by the changes aware? ☐

Is there a channel for receiving improvement ideas from anywhere in the organisation? ☐

Will action be taken on improvement ideas? ☐

Is there a mechanism for dealing with defects if they arise and for re-checking the risks of assumptions? ☐

Process Benchmarking

One tool to help you achieve process improvement is benchmarking. I like to call this "creative theft." In essence, it is about finding someone who does something better than you do, learning how they do it and then setting goals to improve so that you achieve the same performance. You then innovate in some small way so that your performance actually exceeds the other guy. As a notable American business leader once remarked, "People seldom improve when they have no other model but themselves to copy from."

Remember that we are talking about process benchmarking, not product benchmarking. With product benchmarking you will compare your product with that of your competitors; with process benchmarking you are comparing your process with anyone who runs a similar one – they may or may not be your business competitors.

The business implications of this fact are considerable. With process benchmarking, you have available to you a huge source of improvement ideas – far greater than if you only watch your own industry. This provides you with the opportunity to attain very radical improvements. For example, all manufacturers are occasionally asked by customers to "deliver ASAP!". The best rapid delivery processes in the world are not just better than manufacturers can achieve; they are orders of magnitude better. Consider the air ambulance service delivering hospital services on demand in minutes, consider the British armed forces deploying thousands of people and tons of equipment to remote parts of the world in days, consider NASA delivering packages to the most hostile environments anywhere. If the manufacturer can translate these abilities into his own environment and make them appropriate, his improvement would be unprecedented.

However, there are some dangers with benchmarking which you should avoid.

Firstly, it is very easy to copy someone else without really understanding what it is you are copying. Falling into this trap will create a process that looks like the other guy's, but fails to deliver the same value. An example of this, during the 1980s, was the importation of Quality Circles to the West from Japan. Some Western companies did get value from them, but most who tried – didn't. Another example of such behaviour is the way in which a number of companies have implemented BS EN ISO9001 (which is further explained in Chapter 6). They have suffered all the pain but gained little, if any, of the benefit.

The second significant danger of benchmarking is the creeping paralysis of over-complication. The temptation is to study the other guy in ever more detail by developing complex, rigidly controlled procedures for data capture, but to avoid committing yourself to any real action. As the aphorism has it, "Obstacles are those dreadful things you see when you take your eyes off the goal." A sharp illustration of this point was made to a European management delegation who were on a fact-finding visit to major companies in Japan. In one company the President, having been outstandingly free with information about his company's strategies, plans, processes, and systems, was asked by one of the delegates (from a European competitor company) how he could risk being so open. The President replied that it would take the European company ten years to understand what they had been shown and translate it into their own business, by which time his own company would have progressed yet further ahead. The sting was in the tail. "But of course . . ." he said, "my main reason is that I know that you won't do it."

If you fall into this trap, you are then likely to fall into another one. The temptation is to ensure that more people in the organisation learn from this source of new and highly detailed information by developing ever more comprehensive internal communication channels. Remember that studying how to improve something doesn't actually improve it. Benchmarking does not improve anything; it is an investment made in helping you get ideas about how to improve. This over communication of overly detailed competitive data is another form of "paralysis by analysis", only this time it has become a team game. With everyone studying the information in ever more detail, so there are ever more good reasons why taking any proposed action would be wrong and why taking action now would be untimely. The evidence of this problem is widespread, as managers who say things like, "We are constantly faced by great opportunities brilliantly disguised as insoluble problems," would no doubt testify.

The third danger is that once you have attained "the best", you will stop improving. This temptation is compelling because you don't want to invest in over-engineering. But this thinking gives rise to two problems.

The first problem is that once you are "the best" there is no one out there to watch – they're all watching you. So, when someone else overtakes you, you are not watching; and so you lose any advantage you had previously gained.

Producing best rubbish is not enough.

The second problem is that "the best" is only relative to other producers, it takes no account of the perceptions of the customer. If everyone in the world produces rubbish, you producing the best rubbish is not enough.

Benchmarking is not a universal panacea, but don't let the dangers put you off doing it. Benchmarking, if used with thought and managed sensibly, can be an extremely valuable source of improvement ideas and can have a major effect on the speed with which your organisation can improve.

CHANGE THROUGH PROCESS MANAGEMENT
A Summary For Browsers

The World of Change
★ Recognising the need for improvement is the starting point.
★ Customers constantly demand more.
★ Customers constantly demand better value.
★ The challenge that faces your organisation is the customer demand for more, better, cheaper.
★ To satisfy demand your organisation must change and change constantly.

How Do You Deliver Value?
★ Juran's "Trilogy" for quality – "Planning, Control, Improvement."
★ Crosby said, "Prevention is learning to do it right first time" leading to "Zero Defects."
★ Every single output from your business comes from a process.
★ Invest time and effort to understand the process value chain better.

The Process Rule-base
★ Process planning.
★ Requirements.

★ Process engineering.
★ A structured approach.
★ Process control.
★ Measuring and monitoring.
★ Process improvement.

Process Benchmarking
★ "Creative theft."
★ Process benchmarking, not product benchmarking.
★ Never copy someone else without really understanding what it is you are copying.
★ The danger of creeping paralysis of over-complication.
★ Take care – once you have attained "the best", you will stop improving.
★ If everyone in the world produces rubbish, you producing the best rubbish is not enough.

4

CHANGE THROUGH
SYSTEMATIC CORRECTION

In a perfect world all processes would work reliably and be controlled effectively. In a perfect world defective outputs would never occur. Error-free describes the aspirations of a quality organisation.

In the real world, it is extremely rare to attain completely error-free operation but the dissatisfaction, caused by one's failure to do so, is a personal and organisational driver for continuous improvement. We are back to the example I cited in Chapter 1:

— How many mistakes do you make in the average day?
— How many do you want to make?

In the real world, things go wrong. When they do, we must put them right and put them right in such a way that they don't go wrong in the same way again. To do this we must adopt a formal and systematic approach that leads to effective and complete corrective action. A short-term fix is simply not sufficient.

Corrective action is all about repairing processes so that they operate to the required standards and within the required tolerances. Traditionally, when a fault occurs, a quick fix is implemented. This fix often acts not upon the process itself, but upon the output from the process. For example, if a machining process is designed to cut a plate one inch square, but has a defect such that one dimension is 1.2 inches, a fix might be to shave the long side back to one inch. The problem with this approach is that unless the process itself is re-designed, defective outputs will occur again and again. The additional shaving operation means that the costs of the overall process escalate. Repairing the process itself properly may cost money up-front but will invariably be cheaper in the long term. This vision doesn't just apply to manufacturing processes but to any process. Can you think of anything that is cheaper to do wrong the first time and then put right later?

Look around your work place to see how many examples of staff repeatedly fixing things you can find. Some of them could horrify you. Here are just a few of the hundreds of examples I've noticed (and I bet there have been thousands I haven't).

The machinist who removed a safety guard to enable him to access some part of the work.

The restaurant that placed a folded napkin under a short table leg – after the wine had been spilled into the customer's lap.

The truck driver at speed on the motorway wiping the windscreen, because the demister was broken.

The company that had a Complaints Department. (There are dozens of these, some employing more than 100 people – at a cost of over £20,000 per person per year. That is a lot of money!)

Corrective action, to be effective, must be performed in a controlled and systematic way. The first, and most important, stage is to define exactly what problem you are trying

COMPLAINTS DEPARTMENT

The company had a Complaints Department!

to solve. This is frequently done without sufficient care. Often, people express problems emotionally or incompletely, or in terms of someone else's fault, or in such a way as to assume the answer. Consider the following; have you heard people say things like this to define a problem?

"The flipping thing never works on cold mornings."
What is meant by the word never? What is cold? Does it only fail in the morning? The expletive probably indicates a lack of clear thinking.

"Oh I don't know, it won't work that's all."
Has it ever worked or has it ceased to work? The turn of phrase indicates a closed mind and an unwillingness

to find out more. Not only is the speaker unlikely to solve the underlying problem, but will probably be a damn nuisance to anyone else who tries.

"You know your problem, your swing is no good."
The "swing" might or might not be adequate for the task, but by assuming that this is the cause the speaker precludes investigation of any other causes (mis-aligned club, incorrect foot placement, sudden adverse wind, etc.). The problem was actually that the ball did not end up where it was intended. The speaker also uses the accusative, personalising the problem. The effect of this is that the poor golfer now feels threatened and may feel obliged to defend his position. He might say something like "Well, I never play seriously, it's only a bit of fun," thus closing his mind to the prospect of improving. As Sherlock Holmes said, "To theorise before the facts is a capital offence!"

Defining a problem should be done formally and objectively. The following is a guide:

"The **xyz** *process is designed to yield* **abc** *output. On* **n** *of the last* **m** *occasions it yielded* **www**. *We will know that the problem has been corrected when . . ."*

Once the problem is formally defined, the next stage is to plan for its investigation and subsequent resolution.

How significant is the problem?
This helps you set the priority for resolution.

How complex is the problem?
This helps you decide your level of investment.

To theorise before the facts is a capital offence.

What skills are needed to investigate the problem?

How long do you reasonably expect the investigation to take?

At this stage (not before) you can implement a temporary fix if necessary. It is vital that you do not implement the fix before completing the definition of the problem and its investigation plan. If you do, the situation will have changed and securing the information necessary for the definition and plan may be impossible. That being said, you should recognise that there may be considerable pressure upon you to fix the problem quickly – "*When you are up to your neck in alligators it can be a bit difficult to remember that your objective is to get out of the swamp!*"

Assuming that you have resolved the dilemma of formally defining the problem **before** implementing the fix (**immediately**), you will have the necessary information to enable you to start the investigation into a permanent resolution of the problem. The investigation stage involves all the data capture, analysis, theorising and testing needed to identify the underlying cause. While many techniques have been developed to help with cause analysis, most situations call for the application of very few of them. Some of the more widely used techniques are summarised in the next chapter.

Once the underlying cause of the problem has been identified, the process may be re-engineered to eliminate the problem permanently. But this is not the end of the story. The final activity which must be done (and sadly is too often neglected) is to evaluate the solution. Go back to the original problem definition.

— Have you addressed the real problem?
— Have you demonstrated that you have actually solved it?
— Is the solution complete and permanent?

In other words, the whole corrective action process needs to look something like this:

— Define the problem
— Plan for resolution
— Implement a short-term fix if needed
— Find the underlying root-cause
— Implement a permanent correction
— Evaluate the resolution
— Ensure the resolution is permanent.

Clearly, to run such a process inside your organisation, you could just tell all your staff how to approach problem solving and leave them to get on with it. Of course, they won't get very far.

As well as needing a formal, structured approach to solving problems, you also need a formal, systematic approach to managing the solving of problems. You need a system of management, which will guide and support the correction groups running throughout the organisation.

This management system will need to ensure that correction groups are:

— Formed
— Trained
— Resourced (e.g. time off from the day-job, budget, equipment, etc.)
— Given, or required to produce, clear terms of reference
— Monitored
— Given authority to implement solutions
— Provided with support to remove barriers to progress
— Given recognition upon success
— Etc.

Again, the message is clear. Design a formal system in your organisation to ensure the effective and objective management of problems, then train everyone in the organisation to use it effectively. If you don't, your failures will cost you a fortune and your customers will be less than pleased.

CHANGE THROUGH SYSTEMATIC CORRECTION
A Summary For Browsers

★ Permanent elimination of faults, not quick fixes.
★ Problem definition must be formal and objective.
★ Fixes keep you alive while you invest in a complete solution.
★ Re-engineer the failing process, not the faulty product.
★ Check against formal definition to confirm solution correct and effective.
★ Corrective action requires investment.

5

THINK CHANGE TECHNIQUES

Process Modelling Techniques

Given my earlier emphasis on the need to prevent problems and the need for well managed and controlled processes to achieve this, it is perhaps natural that the first techniques in this chapter are to help in Process Modelling. In fact, I am going to describe three techniques: Process Requirement Diagrams, Process Flowcharts and Process Flow Diagrams.

Process Requirement Diagrams

Process Requirement Diagrams are used to help ensure that all the customer's requirements have been defined before the process is developed. In the case of failing processes, they can be used to go back and check that the problem is not one of missing requirements. The outline diagram looks like Fig. 2 overleaf.

The first task when constructing such a diagram is to define the process scope. Where/when does the process start and end? Consider a simple example, the requirements for making a cup of coffee. What is the starting point of this process? Does it start with you getting the coffee jar out of the cupboard, or does it start with you buying the coffee from the shop, or with the shop getting it from the warehouse, or with the refining company, or the shipper, or the grower?

Once the process scope has been decided, the next stage is to list all the requirements under each heading. For example, considering "consumables" alongside process scope enables us to determine whether we are making fresh ground coffee or instant and whether we are starting with pre-ground coffee or with roasted beans.

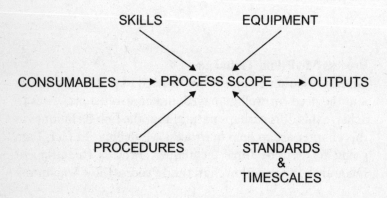

Fig. 2. Outline Process Requirement Diagram.

In my experience, there are three effective uses of Process Requirement Diagrams. The first and second, I have already mentioned, are used as an aid to producing requirement lists for process design and for problem investigation. In these cases there is no great advantage in producing a neatly drawn and elegant diagram; what matters is the completeness of the data. The third use of the diagram, which I have found to be valuable, is as a communication tool to explain to others what your process actually does. In this case, completeness of data is less critical, but a neat diagram is most helpful.

Process Flowcharting

The essence of Process Flowcharting is to use diagrammatic symbols joined by link lines to represent the flow of activity within a process. For example:

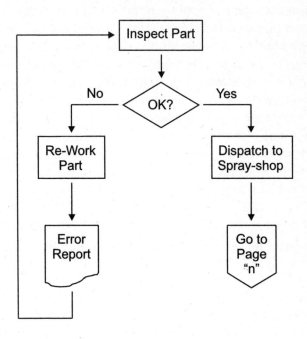

Fig. 3. Process Flowchart.

Process Flowcharts have been in use for decades. Specialists in the field of work-study and industrial engineering often use them to good effect. They have also been widely used for many years in the world of systems analysis and computer programming. In this case the flowchart is used to represent a business process, which is being developed to operate within an information technology environment.

Given the nature of computers (i.e. they are very stupid and only do the steps they are given), a detailed step-by-step guide to the process is a highly valuable stage in translating the human process into computer usable form.

The value of Process Flowcharts as a non-specialist general management tool for improvement is limited. They are complex and time-consuming to produce and, except for the simplest of processes, they are difficult to interpret.

However, one area of improvement management where flowcharts are helpful, especially if they are not produced in too fine detail, is as a diagrammatic representation of the behaviour of an organisation and how the various groups and departments interact. In this case, the flowchart is often a useful first step in business process re-engineering and/or re-organisation.

A problem frequently encountered when producing such flowcharts is that it is not easy to maintain consistency of detail. Any symbol box could itself be broken down into a flowchart and there is no simple way of deciding when the level of detail is right and when it isn't.

Process Flow Diagrams
A Process Flow Diagram is a bit like an amalgam of the Process Flowchart and the Process Requirements Diagram, enjoying the combined benefits of both techniques and avoiding some of the weaknesses.

It is a simple graphical technique for representing process detail and showing interdependencies between subprocesses. It is also an effective communication tool. Except for specialist applications, it is more generally useful than Process Flowcharting and it conveys more information than a Process Requirements Model. Once learned and practised, it can be produced in minutes on a bit of scrap paper. Its design lends itself to representation on computer and its structure enables it not just to capture requirements and flow, but also sequence and parallelism (i.e. parts of the process operating simultaneously). One area in which the technique is weak is that representations of feedback loops can be messy and this must be borne in mind.

The Process Flow Diagram is made up of "Units" each one of which looks like this:

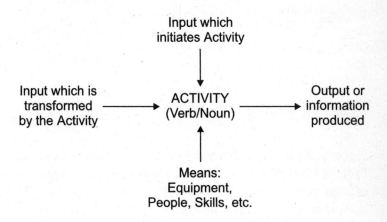

Fig. 4. Process Flow Diagram.

Units are linked together either by their "Outputs" becoming the "Inputs" to the next "Activity", or by the completion of one Activity being an "Initiator" for the next (or both). For an example, see Fig. 5 overleaf.

In this example, the Draft Specification arising from the Activity "Prepare Specification" acts as an Initiator for the "Approve Specification" Activity and is also an Input to it.

In this way a flow of Activities can be represented

showing how each stage is initiated. If process flow is the desired area for study (as in the simple example above), the "Means" can be omitted. If requirements need to be clarified, then the Means should be shown. These Means may previously have been decided using the Process Requirements Diagram.

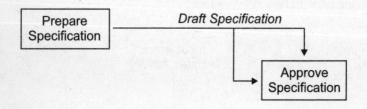

Fig. 5. Linking units together.

As we have seen, Process Requirements Diagrams and Process Flowcharts do not lend themselves to scoping the process description. It is easy to be inconsistent. This technique solves this problem by specifying, as follows, how it should be drawn on the page.

A full Process Flow Diagram should be drawn on a single piece of A4 paper in landscape orientation and should comprise no more than five Units.

From this simple rule, a hierarchy of diagrams may be produced in ever more detail. For instance, a very high-level diagram for a company might have units whose Activities (verb + noun) include Research Product, Develop Product, Sell Product, Support Product, and Withdraw Product. This, in a very simple form, is the generic product lifecycle. The next set of pages (five in total) might break each of the high-level Activities into a further five steps. For example, Research Product might be broken down into Identify

Market, Articulate Needs, Analyse Competition, Set Constraints, and Prototype Product. Each of these Units could itself be broken down into further diagrams.

It is possible to use this technique to describe every Activity in the organisation and show every interrelationship between each Activity and its sub-Activities from high-level organisation-wide operations diagrams to detailed work instructions for individuals. Each diagram can be indexed and cross-referenced and each diagram may be rapidly understood.

This technique, or other proprietary techniques like it, is a cornerstone of Business Process Re-engineering.

Brainstorming

This technique is used as a catalyst to idea generation within a group. It can be used in any context where a list of ideas is the desired outcome (e.g. a list of: problems, possible causes, circumstances, possible remedial actions). It is one of the most well known techniques in the world and one of the most simple. Sadly, it is rare for it to be done properly and so realise its true potential. The brainstorming process starts with the selection of one member of the group to the position of Group Leader. The Group Leader must have complete control and authority of the group during the brainstorming session. His specific role is to capture the ideas as they arise, while the remainder of the group – in strict rotation – offer ideas. Members at their turn may "pass", but may offer another idea when their turn comes round again. The brainstorm is completed once the list is agreed to be long enough for the purpose or all members have passed. At no stage during the brainstorm is it permitted to comment upon the ideas offered, as this would act as a deterrent to members offering apparently silly ideas. The concept of silly ideas is important, as these ideas often turn out not to be silly at all and/or act as a further catalyst to the creation of better ideas.

Pareto Analysis
Wilfredo Pareto was a 19th century Italian economist who discovered a relationship between wealth and its distribution such that 80% of wealth was owned by 20% of the population. From this discovery the name of Pareto has been ever since associated with the ratio 80:20. Once people observed that this ratio occurred again and again, the term "80/20 Rule" was coined which in turn was attributed to Pareto. For example:

— About 80% of complaints tend to come from about 20% of the customers.
— About 80% of the cost of poor quality is attributable to about 20% of the problems in a company.
— About 80% of problems tend to come from about 20% of the possible causes.

A Pareto Analysis involves collecting data to represent the situation and showing this on a bar chart where most frequent occurrences appear on the left and less frequent appear in sequence. The data collection process must be planned with extreme care to ensure that the data gathered is truly representative. Fig. 6 opposite is a simplified example.

The main use of Pareto Diagrams is to help the team focus and set goals for improvement. It is usually easier to reduce a bar's height than to eliminate it completely, so the Pareto Diagram can show where best to invest effort for maximum return. A Pareto Diagram, being very easy to interpret, is also an effective communication tool.

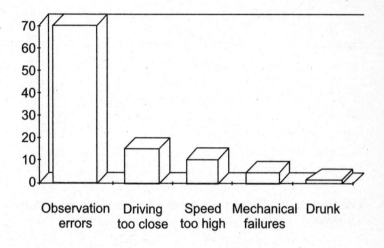

Fig. 6. Pareto Diagram: Causes of "Type x" Car Accidents.

Cum Lines

A variation of the Pareto Diagram is the addition of a "Cum Line" or cumulative line. To generate this from a Pareto Diagram, imagine that all the bars are stacked one on top of the other in column 1 and mark this point. In column two remove column 1's bar, but leave the rest in place and mark this point. Repeat this process for all bars. Fig. 7 overleaf shows this.

The Cum Line is useful for showing improvement. By showing the Cum Line at the start and the Cum Line after action has been taken the gap between the two lines indicates the improvements made. Like the Pareto Diagram itself, it is easy to interpret and is another useful communication device.

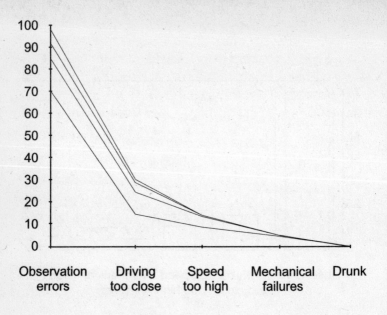

Fig. 7. Pareto Cum Line Diagram: Causes of "Type x" Car Accidents.

Cause and Effect Diagrams

This technique is, in some ways, like brainstorming, but is more structured. It is used in the identification of possible causes. To use the technique, first write the problem – the effect, in a box on the right hand side of a large sheet. Then draw a long horizontal arrow pointing at this box from the left. Then draw four arrows intersecting the horizontal arrow and label these.

Frequently the labels will be "**manpower, machines, methods** and **materials**" but occasionally it may be more useful to label them differently. For example, design, development, testing, and use.

The Cause and Effect Diagram skeleton should look a bit like that of a fish with the head as the effect and a spine with four rays coming into it, two at the top and two at the bottom. Hence its other name – Fish-bone Diagram. A brainstorm is conducted for each of the headings and the ideas captured along the appropriate ray.

Developing the car accident example further, the Cause and Effect Diagram could look something like this:

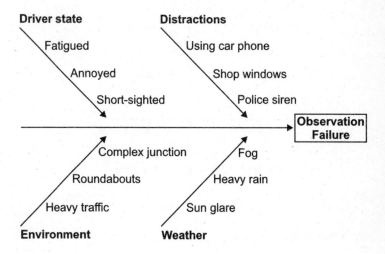

Fig. 8. Cause and Effect Diagram.

SWOT Analysis
This too is a structured brainstorming technique and is used most frequently to analyse the areas of strength and weakness within an organisation, or a business, or a process. By deciding which features are strong, which are weak, where the threats are and what opportunities could be exploited, a plan can be developed to make targeted improvements. This technique is often used as part of the process of strategic planning and/or organisation planning.

The results of the brainstorm are captured on a chart like the one shown below. The brainstorm is conducted in five sections. A brainstorm round is done for Strengths, then Weaknesses, then Opportunities, and then Threats. (The order being decided by the leader to be the most appropriate.) The fifth brainstorm round is conducted for the chart as a whole. Participants are invited to add items wherever they choose.

Strengths   **Weaknesses**

Opportunities   **Threats**

Fig. 9. SWOT Analysis.

Boston Square – Cost/Benefit Analysis
The Boston Square or cost/benefit analysis is used to equate the potential value of a course of action against the cost of taking the action. It therefore is a valuable tool to determine priorities. There are four possible outcomes from the analysis:

The course of action costs little, but has high value.
The course of action costs a lot, but has high value.
The course of action costs little, but has low value.
The course of action costs a lot, but has low value.

The square below shows how these are mapped. Clearly, in most cases, if a proposed course of action costs little but has high value, it should be done first and well. However, experience shows that actions in this category often suffer from a lack of management attention (as implementation has little cost implications) and in consequence fail to be done properly through a lack of supervision or control. In the case of actions with little value and high cost, it is usually sensible not to perform the action at all. However, many such actions are taken because the cost/benefit analysis was not done before the start. Low benefit and low cost actions are potentially very valuable to an organisation; not in themselves, but as a mechanism for people development. For example, such a project could be given to a junior team to help them develop skills, safe in the knowledge that any mistakes they make (people who are learning make more mistakes) will have a low impact.

High   **(Contribution to growth)**   **Low**

	High	Low
High	Should be supported	"Lemon" kill it!
Low	Nurture and protect Ensure focus maintained	"Harmless" review it

Demand on resources

Fig. 10. Boston Square.

Affinity Diagrams

This is another structured brainstorming technique used in group situations. There is no correct way to produce these, so instead I shall illustrate a method that has worked very well for me. It is best described through an example.

A management team comprises a group of twelve departmental managers under a director. The director wants to improve the perception of the organisation in the eyes of the customers and therefore has launched a Customer Care programme. The managers have all been trained in the principles and have bought-in to the concepts. They now wish to devise some projects they can implement that will make a difference. They need to set an example to their staff, so wish to implement the projects themselves (i.e. without delegation). They cannot select too many projects, because experience shows that if they do, they will get swamped with extra work and the projects will get repeatedly traded out. They call in a facilitator to help.

The facilitator gives each manager five sheets of paper (Post-it notes work very well). Each manager silently brainstorms project ideas onto his papers. The "smarty pants" with lots of ideas asks for, and is given, six more papers. The "slow-coach" has only got three ideas, when the facilitator asks the group to stop.

The facilitator asks for the first idea and confirms that the whole group has heard it and understood it. This is then stuck onto the wall (white-board or similar). The facilitator then asks if anyone else has the same or similar ideas. If so, these are stuck near to the first (an affinity). The second idea is then taken and explained, and stuck on the wall away from the first idea (and its affinities). Again, similar ideas are grouped around it. This continues until all ideas are stuck up. While all this was going on "slow-coach" had another idea and this was included, and "smarty pants" realised some of his ideas were unhelpful, so he didn't offer them for inclusion. The wall now had sixty-two papers stuck on it, in twenty-one groups.

An un-led, un-structured discussion of ten minutes exactly.

The facilitator then told the managers that he was going to ask them to stand up and walk to the wall and in an un-led, un-structured discussion of ten minutes exactly, they could move the papers around to reflect the affinities and feelings and consensus of the group better. This was then done. The wall now had sixty-one papers stuck on it, in twenty-five groups.

The next task was to give a descriptive name (six words

maximum) to each affinity set (even if it was a set of one). In this case there were twenty-five of them. These were captured on paper sheets and stuck onto a white-board.

The completed affinity diagram was not nice and neat on a sheet of paper. The raw ideas were stuck in groups all over a wall and the affinity set names were stuck all over a white-board. The managers wanted a permanent record of their deliberations so far, so a copy of the walls and white-board was taken to paper for later reference. (Note: This desire for a permanent record is typical, but once taken it is seldom used again.) The facilitator then used another technique . . .

Metta-planning
This technique is used in group situations when a high level of consensus, and buy-in is required. It is used typically to identify priorities or important sub-sets. The example continues . . .

He asked the managers how many projects they thought they could successfully work on, given their existing workloads. The twelve managers concluded that four projects run by three people per project would be ideal.

The facilitator then gave each manager five, green (as it happens), sticky labels (dots) and told them that these dots represented votes. They could distribute their five votes as they wished – all five to one project, or one vote to each of five projects, or any other combination. He asked them to stand up again, and cast their votes by sticking the dots to the appropriate pieces of paper (each of which contained the affinity summary) on the white-board.

When this was done the papers were rearranged in order of popularity. And a line was drawn underneath the fourth paper. The distribution of dots was very clear. The top four had between them the vast majority of votes; the fifth paper had enough votes to look like a "good back-up" project if any of the first four became untenable. The remaining twenty papers had a few or no votes.

The trick that the facilitator used was to give each delegate one more dot than the desired number of projects. He knew that by doing this, it was statistically likely that the desired number of projects would be selected by the group, with an approximately evens chance of a "good fall-back" project being identified too.

The delegates had a high feeling of involvement throughout and had an equal share of the decision making. The dominant people still felt involved, but didn't dominate and the shy people were involved without being intimidated. The pace of the activities making up the session (affinity diagramming and Metta-planning) enabled the fast thinkers to remain interested, while giving the slower thinkers time to consider.

Statistical Process Control
This is a specialist set of techniques used mainly in manufacturing. It is concerned with controlling the process (or machine) which is making the product. It assumes that if the process/machine is good then the yield will be good, thereby eliminating the need to monitor the product by monitoring the process/machine.

A poorly designed product made in a good process would of course pass all the tests. It would just fail in the market. Similarly a poorly designed process may give a completely correct yield but at a cost that made the product non-competitive. So SPC is not the general panacea it was cracked up to be by some business pundits, when it first became popular in Britain in the 1970s and 1980s.

In fact SPC doesn't actually monitor and control processes/machines either. Instead, it uses statistical techniques to sample products; the behaviour of these samples under test being used to draw conclusions about the performance of the process.

Users of SPC may employ two types of chart: "Variable" and "Attribute". A variable chart monitors measurements of product variables, for example length, mass, number of days, etc. An attribute chart monitors the success or failure of a particular attribute of the product, for example Pass or Fail test. Attribute charts do not use measurements in the pure sense of the word, they report on the state of a judgment.

The mathematics underlying the SPC approach is the statistics of variation. In summary, this is based upon the principle that the design parameters of a process must specify the normal and acceptable variation (tolerances). For example, it is physically impossible to measure 1 inch because down at the atomic level the accuracy of the measure is dependent upon the matter used to make the ruler. The phrase '1 inch' actually means 1 inch plus or minus some value. Depending upon the application, this value may be large or small. In silicon chips used in computers and other high-tech electrical equipment, for example, measurements are made with tolerances at the atomic (angstrom) level, whereas most heavy engineering applications have tolerances many thousands of times greater than this. Variation within these tolerances is acceptable and a normal part of the process operation. Within a proven process it is also predictable, so the statisticians tell us, in a "normal distribution," as long as the process is operating normally. If a product goes outside the pre-specified tolerance then this indicates that the process is not behaving normally, so there must be a special cause of failure that can be systematically rectified.

The Recursive "So What?"

This is a technique for identifying benefits for customers, as opposed to features of the product or service. It is most effectively used as a conversation game between two people and takes only a few minutes. With practice a person can play both sides of the conversation alone.

Person A states a feature of the organisation's product (or service).
Person B takes on the role of imaginary customer and says, "So what?"
Person A then has to answer the question in the form of a benefit – "So you will . . .".
Person B then gets tougher and asks, "So what?" again.
Person A answers again – "So that means that you . . .".

The game continues until Person B is convinced that he, as a customer, would be satisfied. Both Person A and B have now derived a list of benefits for the feature.

Not only can this technique be used in a sales or marketing organisation (which was where it was created), but it can be used as preparation for any situation in which someone needs to be persuaded of the value of something.

The Recursive "Why?"

This technique is sometimes known as the "Five Whys" because Toyota, who branded it as a technique, believed that asking "Why" five times was required to identify the root cause of a problem. This is too dogmatic for me, hence my use of the term "recursive" without any guide as to how often.

It is a very simple technique, but is also very powerful.

First state a problem and then ask why it happens. Then ask why the answer is what it is and repeat the questioning cycle until either the questioner or the answerer believes s/he has gained new insight.

Three-year-olds frequently do it as a game.

Of course, it's far too grand to call this a technique, three-year-olds frequently do it as a game to help themselves manipulate language – or drive mum and dad bonkers!

THINK CHANGE TECHNIQUES
A Summary For Browsers

★ Process Requirement Diagrams.
★ Process Flowcharts.
★ Process Flow Diagrams.
★ Brainstorming.
★ Pareto Analysis – The 80/20 Rule.
★ Cum Line charting.
★ Cause And Effect Diagrams.
★ SWOT Analysis.
★ Boston Square.
★ Affinity Diagrams.
★ Metta-planning.
★ Statistical Process Control.
★ The Recursive "So What?"
★ The Recursive "Why?"

6

CHANGE THROUGH QUALITY SYSTEMS

Quality, we have seen, is the product of clear definition, careful planning, process management and permanent corrective action. When this is being performed in an organisation, a system to ensure all these aspects are controlled is a vital tool. The International Standards Organisation has defined just such a system. In fact they adopted wholesale the British Standards Institution – **BS5750**.

ISO9000 is an internationally recognised standard for quality systems. It requires the definition of the organisation structure, responsibilities, procedures and resources for implementing quality management. This should come as no surprise, as The Process Rule-base, above, requires the same thing.

The history of ISO9000 goes back to the 1970s. The USA military specifications followed by Nato's AQAP standards and the definition of BS5779 (Guidance on Quality Management) were the early forerunners of ISO9000. In 1979 the first contractual standards were introduced as the BS5750 series. These standards were reissued in 1987 and adopted verbatim as ISO9000.

In fact, ISO9000 is a misnomer. It is used colloquially to identify a series of standards and guides as follows:

— ISO9000   Guide to the selection and use of quality systems standards.
— ISO9001   The standard for organisations engaged in design, development, production, installation and servicing.
— ISO9002   A subset of ISO9001 comprising the standard for organisations engaged in production and installation.
— ISO9003   A subset of ISO9001 comprising the standard for organisations engaged in inspection and test activities.
— ISO9004   Guide to quality management and quality system elements.

When most Quality Managers talk of ISO9000, what they really mean is **ISO9001**. In fact, at the end of 1994 this standard was reviewed and edited, and re-branded as BS-EN-ISO900n. But notwithstanding the name, what does the standard actually say?

The standard is in four sections with the first three being preamble. The "meat" is in section 4. This section is in twenty paragraphs, each one specifying standards for an aspect of quality management. For example . . . Section 4.1 specifies requirements under the heading "Management responsibility", 4.2 specifies "Quality Systems" requirements, 4.3 the requirements for "Contract Review". Section 4.4 lays out the standards for design while 4.5 is about documentation. The standard continues with other paragraphs setting requirements for other aspects of quality management, including Process Control (4.9), Corrective Action (4.14), Quality Audits (4.17) and Training (4.18).

In terms of content of these sections, the following quote from the standard illustrates the types of things the standard insists upon.

"4.14 Corrective Action
The supplier shall establish, document and maintain procedures for
a) Investigating the cause of non-conforming product and the correction needed to prevent recurrence.
b) Analysing all processes, work operations, concessions, quality records . . . [etc.] . . . and eliminate potential causes of non-conforming product.
c) . . ." Etc.

In a very (too?) short summary, I suggest that the ISO900n standards require you to: write down what business your organisation is in and who does what. Write down how the processes work (i.e. who are the customers, who are the suppliers, who is the process owner and who operates the process and how the process turns inputs into outputs) and how you ensure that all is working properly and what you do if it isn't.

The Quality Manual you produce should be a document which sets out the general quality policies, procedures and practices of your organisation. The procedures within this manual are documents which define the purpose and scope of an activity and outline what, when, where and by whom the activity is properly carried out. There is a danger here, that in seeking BS-EN-ISO-900n registration, you fall into the trap of creating a bureaucratic monster – documenting everything. The documentation you produce should be the minimum necessary to control your business effectively. For instance, some procedures need not appear in a "dusty old manual" at all. A checklist on the wall of the factory might be more suitable.

To obtain, and then maintain, registration for BS-EN-ISO900n involves more than just producing a documented quality system. Also required is a cycle of audits (both internally and externally conducted) and revisions of the quality systems documentation.

There are two basic types of quality audit – a **system audit** and a **compliance audit**. A system audit determines whether a quality system is in place and is adequate for the purpose. A compliance audit determines whether the quality system is being adhered to. The auditor in both cases is seeking evidence of conformance to the standard.

In a system audit, the auditor might, for instance, start an interview with, "What is the purpose of your workgroup?" and/or, "May I see a copy of the organisation chart which includes you?"

In a compliance audit, the auditor might ask, "It says here in your procedures manual that you chair the . . . monthly meeting, may I see the last four sets of minutes?" In such a case, what he is doing is checking that the meeting takes place and that you chair it – as you say you do in your quality manual. He is also checking that the meeting is controlled and records of conclusions, decisions and actions are captured in proper minutes.

To sum up, securing registration to the standard requires you to do two things: – *say what you do* and *do what you say*.

ISO900n registration is, to many companies, the grail that they seek. There is a belief in some management quarters that "getting BS5750" is the same as "getting quality". Unfortunately this is not the case.

If an organisation has the right approach to quality, then securing accreditation to ISO9001/2/3 is basically simple. If you have already got well managed processes, the documentation you need to comply with the standard should already be in place. If you have a common definition of quality, as I suggested you should have in Chapter 2, you will again already be complying with the standard. Similarly, if you have invested in a formal corrective action process, this meets the requirements of another paragraph in the standard. Let me stress, a well-managed quality organisation can integrate itself into the ISO standard and the standard into it with comparative ease. The organisation that starts with the standard and tries to engineer itself to match is in for a long and expensive haul.

Here is one true story, which nicely illustrates the point. It comes from the research and development division of an international high-technology company and relates to section 4.11 of EN-ISO9001: 1994, which specifies that measuring equipment, must be calibrated.

In one of the development laboratories there was a large anacoustic chamber containing measuring equipment costing many tens of thousands of pounds. To calibrate the equipment (it being highly specialised) it was sent periodically to the National Physical Laboratory where the tests could be performed. This was a highly costly exercise as the accuracy of the calibration was often measured in parts per million. On one occasion a five-kilogram weight was also submitted for calibration and its mass, to an accuracy of thousandths of a gram, was determined. This five-kilogram weight served only one purpose in the laboratory. It was used to hold the door of the anacoustic chamber open to stop it banging. When asked about the calibration, the manager of the unit observed that the ISO quality system said things had to be calibrated and so he'd done just that. When it was pointed out to him that the weight was not used to

Accuracy determined to within thousandths of a gram.

measure anything and that he had just wasted a very
large amount of money, he was somewhat tempted to
give "the whole quality thing" a bad name. It took some
time before he got things back into perspective. Fortu-
nately, in this particular company, this was an isolated
incident and is now a source of some humour – especially to the individual who perpetrated the error. "That
was one of my better cock-ups!" he said.

In the world of Total Quality Management, ISO
standards are just another tool; ISO is not the final
answer. The standard is entirely focused on conformance
quality, and as we shall see in the next chapter, this is
only part of the story. The standards are focused on
control of what you do, but adherence to the standards
will do little to drive continuous improvement and

nothing to help drive competitive advantage. A helpful device? Yes! The grail of quality? Most definitely, no!

CHANGE THROUGH QUALITY SYSTEMS
A Summary For Browsers

★ The ISO 9000 series of standards and guides.
★ Say what you do, and do what you say you do.
★ Use the standards to support your operation, don't make your organisation fit the standard.

7

CHANGE THROUGH CUSTOMERS

So far we have discussed quality in terms of the products and services being offered and the processes which yield them. We have seen that the attainment of quality arises from structured, objective and controlled activities. We have seen that bringing this approach to your organisation and making it second nature is not easy and requires careful planning, constant attention and total commitment from you and your fellow managers and your staff alike. Managers ensure that staff are provided with all the enablers to making quality happen and staff ensure that their personal attitudes, enthusiasms, skills and knowledge are applied with quality in mind. Achieve all this and your products and services will become more reliable, your customers will become happier and your cost base will reduce as you spend less money putting things right.

Suppose you run a restaurant and suppose that your restaurant has got the quality message. Soup that has been salted twice (or not at all) is a thing of the past. No longer are eggs wasted because the soufflés didn't rise and no longer is food prepared twice. Your customers are beginning to say nice things about your food. You even managed to increase your prices by 10% and no one seemed to mind a bit. You are a happy manager. Then one day you get a customer comment, "We loved the food, but it would have been nice if we didn't have to wait ten minutes for the table to be made ready."

Over the following weeks you get more comments: "Great meal, but fresh flowers on the table are so much nicer than artificial." And, "Your soufflé was a triumph! Quite superb! But why do you only offer a cheese soufflé? A plain soufflé would be nice too." And, "Your food is marvellous, but you're always booked up!" You then realise what it is that you are hearing – "*Your quality is so good that we noticed it, but . . .*"

This single statement contains two helpful pieces of information. Firstly, you have made superb progress with your drive for quality improvement. If you start to hear unsolicited praise messages like this from your customers, you just make sure you feel good – you deserve it! Make sure also that your people feel good – they deserve it too! Never forget, and never fail to make fuss about, customer praise. It is the only praise there is that has any real value.

The second helpful message is the "but." You must learn to listen for the "but." Is it being used to complain or is it being used to suggest? For example, is it like this, "Your chips were good, but your fish was awful!"? Or like this, "Your chips were good, but it would have been great if I'd been offered a choice of batter or breadcrumbs on the fish"?

If it is the first, you are still hearing about quality problems, but you should know this anyway. Most customers won't bother using the "but," they'll either tell you straight or they will stop doing business with you.

If it is the second one, you have an opportunity to offer

Your quality is so good that we noticed it, but . . .

your customers a bit extra. You have the opportunity to create a differentiator in your business, safe in the knowledge that the customer wants it. You can start to turn quality management from being a cost containment programme to being a real vehicle for positive competitive advantage – while you save money doing it. And that really is the business equivalent of manna from heaven!

Celebrate when you hear customers start saying "Great! . . . but . . ." and then launch your energies to ELIMINATING THE BUT.

Many of the "buts" will be small and easy to do. Many of them will make your offerings different from your competitors. And any "but" you are seen to react to will, for sure, secure the loyalty of the customer who suggested it. Loyalty is one of the few defences an organisation has against externally driven change. If you can keep your customers loyal you will have the time and the revenue to react.

In general business terms, there is no reason to believe that there will ever be any reduction in the rate of change. History suggests that the reverse is true. All of us are seeing new competitive products coming to market from more suppliers from more countries in the world. Not only are more products entering the market, but they are doing so more rapidly. With the globalisation of mass communications, the announcement and introduction of new products and services is faster than ever before. The increase in global competition inevitably gives rise to margin pressure.

Technologies, all technologies, and the application of them, continue to advance at an ever-faster rate. With more competitors globally comes more innovation. To respond to these new competitive technologies requires capital investment in research, development and production. But, as we all know, investment money becomes harder to find when margins are being eroded. The only practical option therefore is to protect margins by optimising the cost base while sustaining revenue. As more companies focus on the containment of costs and the improvement of product quality, so their ability to differentiate becomes harder. The world is a competitive place – and increasingly so. Making products and services that deliver what was promised is increasingly becoming the norm. Organisation after organisation throughout the world is taking quality more seriously and so quality alone is becoming less of a differentiator.

Your business must achieve two things: reduce failure costs by making things right first time and also retain your existing customers by securing their long-term loyalty. The conclusions from independent market research studies are unequivocal:

—   It costs on average five times more to win a new customer than keep an existing one.

—   A retained customer will spend on average five times more with you than a new one.

—   A happy loyal customer is likely to recommend you to up to five of his friends.

—   Only five per cent of unhappy customers will tell you that they're unhappy – the others just won't do business with you again.

—   Unhappy customers are likely to tell fifteen of their friends of their experiences and advise them never to do business with you either.

The trick then is loyalty. Loyalty is a human emotion. Structure, control and objectivity are unlikely to achieve it. What is needed is a "human face" to the enterprise. People buy from people; they do not buy from companies. People make friends with people not companies. Customer Care is the personal touch, which pleases the customer so much that s/he is willing to do business with you again.

By contrast:

—   Are you suspicious of a company that has a Customer Care line for their customers to use when they have queries?

—   Are these companies generally too slow to answer it?

—   Have you observed calls to the Sales Office being answered faster than calls to the Customer Care department?

—   Is it just me, or do you get irritated by a Customer Care line that is answered by a machine?

—   Are you even more cross when a machine answers your call just to tell you to hold-on? You are now paying for the call, the ringing tone tells you to hold-on too – but at least it's free.

— Does the person who answers the phone use an obviously pre-scripted greeting (usually at fifty words a second) in which they give you just a Christian name – so that you know you'll never be able to ask for that person again? Does this strike you as lacking a certain something?

— Do you ever get referred to as "Sir" and feel they meant to say "cur" or "Madam" and feel they meant "madman"?

— Do you feel that when junk mail is addressed to you by name the company who sent it is being impertinent?

— Do you ever ask to speak to someone in higher authority?

If you answered "Yes" to any of these questions (or many others like them) you have experienced a company that is profoundly and fundamentally missing the point. Customer Care is not an institutionalised business process. It cannot, by definition, be automated. An organisation simply cannot go through the motions and expect customers to fall for it.

While sitting at my desk writing this section on Customer Care, the post arrived. Amongst it, came the sort of nonsense that shows what not to do.

It was a letter from the marketing department of the building society which had previously supplied me with a mortgage. This mortgage I had repaid when I moved house. (A common enough situation.) My new house has a mortgage supplied by a different lender. (Again, nothing unusual in that.) The letter from this marketing department was addressed – yes, you've guessed it – to my old address.

MARKETING DEPARTMENT

Their sole purpose in life is to annoy me.

Not content with this piece of crassness, the marketing department went one better. (*You know there are days when I feel that all marketing departments are staffed entirely by irritating maggots whose sole purpose in life is to annoy me – I know this is entirely unreasonable and I know that not all marketing departments are bad and not all marketers are fools. But there are days . . . Or is it just me?*)

Anyway, inside the mis-addressed envelope was a survey produced by a market research company on behalf of the building society. (*You know there are days when I feel that all market research organisations are staffed entirely by . . .* Sorry, you know the rest!)

Question one, quite sensibly, asked me to confirm that I had either obtained a new mortgage or repaid a mortgage with the building society. I answered "Yes".

The next question asked me to indicate which ONE statement was true of: (a) Bought first property, (b) Obtained new mortgage, and moved house, (c) Obtained new mortgage, but didn't move house, (d) Repaid mortgage and have not taken out a further mortgage. In my case, both questions (b) and (d) applied – I have obtained a new mortgage and have moved house, I have repaid my mortgage with them and have not taken another mortgage out with them. Exit one survey in a puff of logic.

The next question was: "Thinking about your previous mortgage, how long had you had it?" My previous mortgage was with them, so they must have known the answer. Perhaps they were deliberately trying to make it *one of those days when I feel that all marketing departments are staffed by . . .*

I then got to question seven, where they asked who my previous mortgage was with! From the fact that they had thought to ask question one, they knew that, for that percentage of respondents who had paid off their mortgage, this question was bound to irritate. (As were questions 3, 4, 5 and 6.) The previous lender of a paid off mortgage must be the lender doing the survey. *You know there are days . . .*

Instead of completing the survey and returning it in the pre-paid envelope (one hopes, correctly addressed!), or simply getting irritated and throwing the whole lot in the bin (which is what most of us would do), I decided to try to be constructive and positive. I annotated the letter and the survey form, addressed a new envelope to the Quality Director of the Building Society and sent it to him, along with an accompanying letter, (reproduced below) which offered my services as a consultant. (Well, ya gotta try haven't you?)

[date]

Dear Sir,

I am concerned that your marketing department and market researchers may be doing your organisation a disservice. Instead of returning the survey and letter to the researchers, I have sent it to you with a few rough notes which I hope you find helpful.

You may also be interested to know that I am a management consultant who specialises in continuous improvement, Customer Care and business excellence and who might therefore be of service to you in future. I have enclosed a short brochure to introduce myself.

Finally, I am currently in the process of writing a book with the working title "The Bedtime Book of Business Excellence and Other Mistakes" as supporting literature for my training courses and possibly for publication. I am considering featuring your recent correspondence in it as an example. I enclose a draft of the chapter. Naturally I do not attribute the example to you or anyone else, as I would never knowingly do harm to an organisation. I am concerned that this story is a bad news story and am sure that you would welcome the opportunity to help me modify it. I would also be delighted to include a positive story about your organisation, believing that it is so much better to praise than to condemn. If you can help me in this, I shall be delighted to hear from you.

Yours faithfully . . .

I have never received either a reply, or even an acknowledgement of receipt. Perhaps they were offended by my comments. I do hope not; I was genuinely trying to be constructive. I suppose that now my chances of securing a consulting assignment from them are not great. But that seems fair enough, because I am absolutely certain that their chance of ever getting my business again is zero!

As a postscript to this story, consider question sixteen. This asked how important was each of a list of features in selecting a mortgage lender. Top of the list was fixed interest rates, next came discount offers. Last on the list was "Excellent Customer Service"! *You know there are days* . . .

The organisations which succeed with their customers are those which employ managers and staff who empathise with them, those who make sure they know their customers, those who try to develop an individual relationship, those who assure them that all will be OK, those who put things right without fuss.

Putting things right in a professional manner is more important than you may imagine. Naturally, you need to put faults right, but by doing so the effect is greater than saving the pain of the problem. If something does go wrong but is put right quickly and well, the customer who suffered the problem is actually more likely to become a loyal customer than the customer who never experienced any problems with you at all. But, never forget that most dissatisfied customers don't complain, so you'll never have the chance to put their problems right unless you observe the problem yourself.

To give a real world example, last year some friends of mine went on holiday to Portugal. Upon arrival at the hotel they were told that there had been an administrative blunder and the hotel had been over-booked, as a result of which, they would be accommodated in the annex. As you can imagine, their hearts sank. However, it turned out that the annex was the luxury extension to the hotel and of considerably higher standard than the hotel itself. The holiday brochure (they had actually brought it with them) showed that staying in the annex added over £150 per person per week to the price of the holiday. The following morning the holiday representative called and asked if £40 would be OK. Again their hearts sank, but they did accept that this represented very good value for money and so agreed to pay the surcharge. "Oh no!" protested the rep. "I didn't mean that! I meant, would you accept £40 each as compensation for us not keeping our promise to you?" Guess from whom they are buying their holiday this year!

As Customer Care is focused upon customers as individual people, there is no limit to the ways in which a positive impression can be created. Customer Care provides you with an infinite opportunity for differentiation.

To illustrate the power of Customer Care, think for a few minutes about your own experiences as a customer. Think of an occasion when a supplier made you so angry that you vowed that you would never do business with him again. Now think again, but this time address your mind to an occasion when, as a customer, you were delighted with the supplier.

In two columns headed "Delighting Factors" and "Angering Factors", summarise the situation, how you reacted to it, how the supplier reacted and what you did next. You should end up with a sheet that looks a bit like the one overleaf, with your two stories captured in answer to the questions in each column.

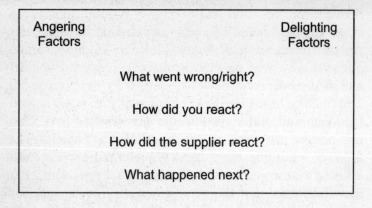

Fig. 11. Analysing Angering and Delighting Factors.

If you look at the two lists of answers, you should notice that the "Angering Factors" show tendencies to be specific, tangible and relate to unreliability. The "Delighting Factors" tend to be more focused towards how empathetically you were treated and how responsive the supplier was to your needs. This is not a hard-and-fast rule, but it is generally the case. Normally, it is the people serving the customer who create delight, while it is the products and services that anger them.

Now consider your *expectations* as a customer. Look at the two sets of answers again. You will probably find that the "Delight" story was more of a surprise to you than the "Anger" story. For most of us the story is that good service is even rarer than rocking horse droppings. Tom Peters, that most renowned and entertaining business guru, in a speech once said (actually he shouted it – because he cares), "If you treat your customer with basic, homespun, common-or-garden variety, basic courtesy you can have the lion's share of any market you choose – because you'll be alone!" Little wonder then that, as we expect to be treated badly, when we are not it surprises us so much that we want to make a fuss about it. It just goes to prove how simple it would be for you to make a difference in your market.

Often at the end of one of my talks on quality and Customer Care someone will come up to me with a "now top that" story. Well, I was giving a talk a few years ago to a group of very senior officers from the three armed services. At the end of the session one of them came up to me and said:

"Now I've got the Customer Care story to end all stories. Let me tell it to you; you might be able to use it. It's about the [then] Chief Executive of British Airways, Sir Colin Marshall.

"I was flying out to Guernsey a few months ago to formally open a new Territorial Army unit. So I arrived at the British Airways desk in the full regalia – including ceremonial sword. Now, as you probably know, there are certain items that are prohibited on aircraft for pretty obvious reasons – explosives, for example. Well, another prohibited item is a sword. I knew this, so when I got to the check-in I requested that the sword be handed directly to the Captain for carriage in the flight-deck safe. This is the only place in which such items may legally be carried. The woman on the check-in desk had obviously never encountered this sort of situation before and said to me that it would be all right to put it in the hold. I explained that my sword was very valuable and that it would be inappropriate (not to mention illegal) to carry it in the hold. I suggested that she referred the matter to her supervisor. She had clearly never heard of upwards delegation and so decided to check it out with the man on the adjacent desk. He had never encountered such a situation either, nor did he know about using managers to help him. He too suggested that my sword be put in the hold. By this time my patience was wearing a little thin and so I said, 'Where's Sir Colin Marshall then. Let's ask him.' The response was classic, 'Oh, him . . . he's never around when we need him.' I gave up. My sword was carefully packed in plastic bubble wrap and stored in the hold."

At this point the soldier's story started to describe a series of coincidences which elevated his tale from the merely interesting to the heights of surreal metaphor.

"I sat down in my aisle seat and then noticed that, by pure coincidence, the person next to me across the aisle was none other than Colin Marshall himself. While I don't know Colin Marshall socially, it happens that I had met him at a function a couple of weeks earlier and so he recognised me and we started to chat. I recounted my story of the sword and the check-in and how his airline was currently breaking aviation regulations by carrying it in the hold – we had quite a giggle about it . . . well I did, he seemed a little embarrassed. The flight came to an end and we went our separate ways. A couple of days later, I had opened the T/A Unit and attended a reception with the island's Governor. The time had come for my return to the UK. As I was a guest of the Governor, I was given the full VIP treatment. Chauffeur driven limousine with pennants on the bonnet, straight out onto the tarmac – no check in. Again, by pure coincidence, Colin Marshall had completed his business at the same time and was returning to the UK on the same plane that I was about to use. He was in the Club lounge waiting for the flight to be called; just as the Governor's limousine, with me on-board, swept onto the tarmac. Now I guess that when he saw the limousine with the governor's pennant on it, he added two and two together, or he saw me through the glass, or was just plain psychic. But when the car came to a halt, Colin Marshall was there waiting. He opened the back door, leaned into the car and said to me, 'I'll look after your sword for you, sir – please enjoy your flight.' Well, when the big boss of 'Britain's favourite airline' is so embarrassed by an incident that he delivers service like that personally, I reckon that British Airways are taking Customer Care seriously."

The real point of this story is that when the chief executive of any company is prepared to do something mundane to help a customer, it's a sure signal that he's serious; and when the CEO is serious, other people in the organisation cotton-on pretty quickly and start to follow suit. What's more, outsiders cotton-on too, because stories like that get passed around, eventually joining the folklore of the business. There are countless stories of British Airways taking care of customers, and Sir Colin Marshall taking quality and Customer Care seriously. Their reputation – the folklore – is such that even if a story is not true – many of us hope and expect it to be.

Tom Peters tells other stories about air travel. He describes his own experiences as a passenger. In one story he describes the nightmare of landing in Detroit one wet night when the pilot turned too sharply off the runway and ended up in the mud. Having gunned the engines for a while, he ran out of fuel. Whereupon they attempted to bus the passengers off the plane. The only vehicle available was a six-seat mini-bus, so it took hours before everyone was off. Peters remarks that while the ordeal itself was terrible, what really got to him was the fact that the person who had caused all this grief didn't even bother to walk down the plane to apologise. He tells another story in contrast, about a flight where, having landed at his destination, he discovered that his baggage had been delivered to the wrong country. He observed that he was treated so well by the staff concerned that he ended-up writing to the Chief Executive of the airline to say what a great company he ran. This, despite the laws of physics proving that no matter how well he was treated, his bags were still in the wrong place and would take at least a day to be recovered.

Not all Customer Care stories arise from problems. A few years ago I was attending a conference in Amsterdam and was staying at the Marriott Hotel. It was December and one evening we were regaled with the legends of Saint Nicholas and Black Peter – the Dutch equivalent of our Father Christmas. On the evening when all the Dutch children were getting their presents (which in Holland is earlier in the month than Christmas itself) I went to my room to discover a traditional seasonal gift of a chocolate bar in the shape of an initial on my pillow. My Christian name is Paul; my letter was "P" – coincidence or care? I like to think it was intentional. The gift itself was a nice touch and would have impressed me as an act of Customer Care. But by making it personal, they went one better, which is why I remember the Amsterdam Marriott Hotel warmly.

At the start of this chapter I started with a miserable story from the Financial Services Sector. Let me end the chapter by redressing the balance.

Our house contents insurance is supplied by CIS Insurance Services, who instead of arranging for us to pay our premiums through Standing Order or Direct Debit, send their representative, Colin, round to our house one evening per year. Colin is such a thoroughly straight and decent bloke that we are glad to see him, and we always invite him in for a brew and a chat. Using Colin must cost CIS more than getting payment directly from a bank, but of course, because we see him every year, we review our cover with him every year; so obviously we avoid being under-insured even more carefully. This must mean that CIS are making more revenue, by using Colin, than it costs them to keep him on the road.

What's important though, is that we prefer doing business with Colin. My wife and I trust him. We value his advice. We therefore *want* to carry on doing business with him. This means that we *want* to do business with CIS. Which is odd, because as far as my wife and I are concerned, we've never had any dealings with CIS, we deal with Colin!

It gets better. Conventional wisdom has it that house contents insurance is a grudge purchase. In other words, as long as the supplier provides basically competitive cover, he competes purely on price with his competitors. With CIS we know that the cover is competitive and that the premium is there or thereabout. What we do not know is whether they are the cheapest – we don't look, we want to do business with Colin. What was I saying about "people buy from people"?

All these stories, the holiday in Portugal, the soldier's tale, the Detroit disaster, the wrong baggage, the chocolate bar on the pillow and even good old Colin show the same fundamental truth: *Customer Care is personal, sincere and exceeds expectations.*

Customer Care is sincere and it is personal. Sincere means that your people must do what they think is right. Personal means that customers need to be treated individually.

If you can surprise your customer by giving him the personal touch, which exceeds his expectations, you will win his loyalty. If you try and fake it, institutionalise it, regulate it, or automate it, chances are you will have the opposite effect. The aim with caring for customers is to get them to say "wow!"

CHANGE THROUGH CUSTOMERS
A Summary For Browsers

★ "Your quality is so good that we notice it . . . BUT."
★ Eliminate the "but".
★ Making products and services that deliver what was promised is increasingly becoming the norm.
★ Quality alone is becoming less of a differentiator.
★ People buy from people, they do not buy from companies.
★ Customer Care is the personal touch which pleases the customer so much that he is willing to do business with you again.
★ Customer Care is sincere and it is personal.
★ Exceed expectations – provide the "Ooh, that was nice."

8

THE CULTURAL DIMENSION

Tom Peters wrote of a "Passion for excellence." The term "passion" is well chosen. Making continuous improvement and Customer Care happen in an organisation must be managed and, said Peters, "Managed with conviction, pride, enthusiasm and absolute integrity at all times. Without integrity it all falls apart."

If you are a manager it is what you think, say and do that makes the difference. Most especially, it is what you do that has the most impact. It is your actions that are the most powerful agent for change in your organisation. As many management commentators have observed: "The biggest single factor in driving change is management style."

The principles and ideas behind continuous improvement and Customer Care are straightforward. Unfortunately, too many people see no further than slogans and exhortations. It is only by getting beyond the empty "talking about it" stage and really making the ideas your own that you can translate them from aphorism to a meaningful mission and strategy in your business. F James McDonald, when President of General Motors, reportedly said poignantly: "It's one thing to say that top management is committed but employees are sceptical – what they are looking for is a consistent message, in what you say, or write and even in every action you take."

For example:

— Managers decide how much to invest in training.

— Managers decide how much direct customer contact they and their people have.

— Managers decide how much personal time to dedicate to convincing staff that they are serious about continuous improvement and Customer Care.

— Managers decide if and how to turn suppliers into partners in the enterprise.

— Managers reinforce behaviour by making heroes out of people.

— Managers decide whether to commit investment in systems that correct problems permanently.

— Managers decide whether to invest in process management.

— Managers decide if they want to know about the thousands of little things that could be improved and they decide whether to take any notice when they're told.

We are what we repeatedly do. Excellence is not an act but a habit.

Culture is the fundamental essence of quality, Customer

Care and business excellence. Quality is not a set of tools and techniques, Customer Care is not a recipe for being nice to customers and business excellence is not winning awards and certificates. As Philip Crosby said, "If you ain't got it, you just can't fake it." It has to come from the heart.

It has got to become part of the organisation woodwork. Everyone in the organisation does it because it is the natural thing to do. Joe Goasdoué, former Quality Director of the computer giant ICL, often described quality in the company as, "just the way we do things round here."

The culture of an organisation arises from the signals people in the organisation receive. Behaviour is the most powerful signal of them all. What is done has much more impact than what is said. When developing an organisation to manage change and improvement, every single feature of the business and every single action taken in the business have an impact upon the evolving culture. Of all the actions and signals that affect this culture, none has a greater impact than behaviour which affects the individual's perceptions of job security and job function.

Three, often seen, areas of high impact behaviour are: delayering, downsizing and empowerment. The "chattering classes" of business gurus and consultants have been flaunting these as the cure for all business ills for many years. Tragically, companies have been swallowing the medicine without thought. And, in business, to do anything without thought is a recipe for failure. Let us briefly consider each in turn.

Delayering is the process by which layers of management are removed from the organisation. The principle behind this is that middle managers add little direct value (neither making product nor servicing customers) so, by their removal, bureaucracy will be reduced and hence communications, decision making and customer responsiveness throughout the company will become faster and more effective.

The principle underlying downsizing is, that instead of increasing sales and margins (i.e. organic growth) a company can rapidly improve its profitability by reducing its costs. So, get rid of people and pass their work onto those who remain. By linking downsizing to delayering, the people to get rid of first are supervisors, middle managers and, in big corporations, some senior managers too. The most significant cost inside most companies is that of people.

The scenario continues with empowerment. Senior executives seldom know how to run the day to day operations of the business, and have not got the time to do so, even when they do. As they have removed the managers who run these operations, responsibility for this passes down through the hierarchy to the lowest possible level. Work teams become responsible for their own quality, costs and schedules. Individual worker accountability and hence authority and responsibility increase.

On the face of it delayering, downsizing and empowerment are a sound approach. Indeed, elsewhere in this book I have suggested the need to give workers freedom to act (authority) so that they take for themselves accountability for their actions (responsibility). However, I have also suggested that in business there is no such thing as a sound recipe for anything. Delayering, downsizing and empowerment, like any other business fashion, must be approached with an open and critical mind. Far too many organisations have created for themselves more difficulties than they have solved by adopting this

approach with too much zeal and not enough considera-
tion. Again, let us consider each in turn.

Delayering has soundness at its heart. It is obvious that
in many organisations managers spend far too long in
unproductive meetings with other managers. This leads to
the wry observation that, "A meeting is a place where
minutes are taken and hours are lost." I recently visited a
company whose senior managers, every Tuesday, attended
a Contract Review meeting. Nothing unusual in that you
might say, until I tell you that the company had no
outstanding contracts and an empty order book! Despite
this nonsense, I am pleased to report that this company,
over the next six months, got its act together and is again
trading successfully. Mind you, it was a close call. At one
stage the management team appeared to have lost the will
to live.

Many managers give far too much attention to the
development of pedantic rules, which provide no direct
value to the business. I recently read in one company's
Quality Manual that it was the Technical Director's
responsibility to verify that shop-floor work instructions
are produced, implemented and updated. What!? I wonder if this guy has time to do what he's presumably paid
for? Does he sound like the sort of chap who creates
policy and strategy and who spends his time deep in
thought about the competitive development of new products and services? Do you think he is the sort of
Technical Director that stays awake at night thinking
about reducing costs and increasing revenues through
technological innovation? Or, do you reckon he is an
interfering piece of make-work who just gets up everybody's nose? I bet one thing's for sure: I bet he doesn't
actually do any work on the shop floor. What do you
think? No, I don't know either. I've never met the man

An empty order book.

or seen him work. I've just read the Quality Manual. But, isn't that enough? I feel like I know him already. Which does suggest that there's a lot of him about.

Managers often spend considerable amounts of time receiving and reviewing reports and statistics, but very little time taking any action on what they read.

I was recently serving as a consultant to the MD of a medium-sized medium-tech manufacturing company. While on this assignment, I was chatting to the company Quality Manager. He described to me the collection of reports and statistics he produced for the company board and other senior managers every month. I asked to see a copy and was shown a document of over sixty pages, much of it showing graphs of progress over time. The thing that was instantly apparent was that none of the graphs showed any trends; they were all apparently random. I asked him what action he took on the statistics, to which he replied that it was his job to report what was happening and management's job to make the changes within the operation. Tentatively, I accepted this, but suggested that it was also his job to ensure that his reports were at least read and that his board was aware of what actions were being taken. I then suggested that next month he should produce the report as normal but not issue it to anyone. If he got complaints then he would know that his report was being read. If he got no comments, then he was armed with evidence of a real issue for concern to the main board. So lacking in authority and confidence was the Quality Manager that he was not prepared to take this advice until after I had let the MD in on the plan. The MD incidentally thought that it was a "wizard wheeze" and promised to "go ballistic" at the appropriate time (he knew, just like we did, what would happen). Month-end came and went and the report stayed in the Quality Manager's office. Of the twenty recipients, not a single one noticed the report's non-arrival. The MD, bless him, duly "went off like a bottle of pop."

The problem with delayering is, in my view, that it only addresses a symptom of the problem not the problem itself.

The real issue in business today is that of change; and, to handle this, organisations need to be constantly learning and adapting. To maintain a competitive position requires responsive evolution. What seldom if ever works is turbulence and revolution. Even if the revolution does yield a breakthrough it is unlikely to be trusted for a considerable period (market reticence to accept radical products or worker reluctance to accept radical working practices being just two examples of why this is).

Surprisingly perhaps, senior executives all too often seek step function improvements to product, service, technology, profits, etc. (Could they be seeking a place in the history books?) They talk of "paradigm shifts" (a dubious use of semantics.). Senior executives frequently seek revolution. (The "Quality Fad" in the 1980s was just such a case.)

Revolution inevitably means taking steps back before the leap forward. Current position is sacrificed to the belief that it will be regained and exceeded in future. Sadly, it seldom is. Before the full benefit of the step change has been attained, the next one has been launched and further steps backward are taken.

I must have encountered over fifty managers in the last year who, when talking of "quality", said something equivalent to, "Oh yes, we tried that once, but the wheel fell off." I'm not bloody surprised the wheel fell off! Their organisations had built their "Quality Cart" in six weeks, whereupon the managers started driving it at 100 mph before the glue had dried. The net effect was that they had spent much of the cost but won little, if any, of the benefit. Those companies who took smaller steps, slower, along the quality road secured massive benefit for themselves and their customers.

It is even worse than that! So persuasive is the gung-ho revolutionary approach to business that even some of the winners in the "Quality Management Handicap Stakes" have now given it up for some new craze, despite the certain knowledge derived from actual experience in the company that it was working for them. That is a mis-management and a mis-thinking offence, which is the equivalent of biting the heads of five-day-old pedigree puppies. It is a tragedy that "Jam tomorrow" is such a forceful idea in today's business world that it makes normally intelligent rational people behave like savages towards their organisations.

In other areas, it is the wreckage of broken companies that is the tragic evidence that British organisations are not very good at evolving. Britain's industrial heartland in the West Midlands is quite literally strewn with the wreckage of a once great industrial past. There were car companies that couldn't compete on quality. There was an entire aircraft industry that just gave up trying to compete on price. And, most notably of all, there were motorcycle companies whose quality was the best in the world, but which were decimated by new technology, clever packaging, fierce pricing and, most significantly of all, by their own belief in the invincibility of their position. Every one of these industries, and there are far too many others, failed because they could not evolve.

To create an evolving organisation requires that we learn to maintain and develop and nurture a population of enthusiasts, champions, thinkers, communicators, and idea generators. People, who can, on the one hand, take a step back from the details of actually doing the job, and on the other, apply pragmatism to the elevated statements of strategic direction. We need a population of people who develop and nurture others, who teach and coach. We need a population of seekers and finders who are interested in discovering what is going on outside the organisation and can interpret what they see.

There is one untapped source of all these evolutionary skills: middle management. Above them in the organisation, the pressure for revolution is too great; below them the perception of the big picture is missing.

Unfortunately, for decades we have asked our middle managers to regulate, monitor and control; which, in most organisations, means maintaining the status quo.

Not surprisingly, they created and maintained bureaucracy. For decades middle managers have been intellectually starved, and have been intellectually starving their people.

We must re-think the role of our middle managers, not delayer them out of existence. Middle management should be the intellectual conduit for the organisation, simultaneously translating the language of things and time of the shop floor to the language of concepts and money of the boardroom. They should be the eyes and ears of the company as well as its ambassadors. They should be the evolvers of our organisations not the defenders of the latest fads and fashions. They should be dedicated to enhancing tomorrow, not the status quo of today.

Delayering is based upon sound ideas and many organisations are over managed. But, middle managers have an absolutely fundamental new role. Organisations should think hard about those managers in whom they are really going to invest for the future.

Downsizing too is based upon sound principles. The danger with it is doing too much too fast. This tendency is particularly noticeable in public limited companies where the pressure from shareholders to adopt a zealous downsizing strategy can be considerable. Only by rapid profit rises can dividends be assured and a rapid reduction in headcount leads to just such a rapid rise. Long-term investments for organic growth are much harder to "sell" to shareholders, especially if this is seen to impact dividends. A volatile share price is a real danger to companies as this leaves them exposed to take-over bids and so, to keep the shareholders loyal to the stock, the pressure to provide increasing dividends year on year becomes ever greater.

This reasoning, if taken to extreme, would preclude any

corporate investment in pure research, would act as a brake to technological innovation and lead to company fortunes throwing up real surprises like rapid growth for a number of years followed by a spectacular corporate crash. Actually, we've seen all of these things happening in Britain over the last decade. The downsizing situation already looks somewhat extreme.

Job security is poor.

Of course with the advances in new technology, particularly information technology, organisations can and should become leaner and this may well lead to reductions in headcount. Linked to delayering, the removal of some managers is possible too. But as every factory worker in Britain will tell you "reductions in managers, no matter what explanation is given or what promises are made, always lead to reductions on the shop floor."

But is this true?

It doesn't matter one jot whether it's true or not! That is the perception; and *it is the perceptions of people in an organisation that are the organisation's culture.*

At the start of the chapter, I discussed the importance of actions in cultural development, now we need to add another dimension. It is not the actions themselves that really matter, but it is the *perception and interpretation* of those actions that is the key.

If the perception of the organisation is that job security is poor and "even the managers are getting hit," it is likely that the culture will be consistent with revolution and not supportive of evolution. Continuous improvement starts to sound like at best another fad and at worst a real threat to people's livelihoods.

Finally, we come to empowerment. Of course, we want everyone in the organisation to have the authority and take responsibility for the work done. Of course, we want everyone to identify improvement opportunities and perform experiments and learning tasks to see if they can be attained. Of course, we want managers, workers, executives, men, women to work together as a mutually supportive team. Many companies even go so far as to talk about "being a family." Of course, we want people to feel like they own the organisation. So, what does the average British company do about it?

First they strive for expansion. The best companies, so the accepted wisdom goes, are the biggest ones. Big companies employ tens of thousands of people. How the blazes is anyone expected to feel part of "a family" of thousands? Most of us lesser mortals struggle keeping a family of Mum, Dad, two in-laws, a couple of kids, Auntie Dot and Great Uncle Albert from tearing itself apart. How we are expected to achieve it in a "family" the size of Runcorn defies belief.

Secondly, the managers stand up in front of the staff and "launch" empowerment. They tell them that everyone is now empowered. What happens next is a deafening silence followed by dramatic inactivity. At the first sign of imposed discipline from above, everyone says, "Well, that proves that they were lying," and another corporate management fad dies unceremoniously and unlamented.

The alternative is so much simpler to do, but it is totally alien to the average senior manager. Say nothing and just do it. Do not announce that people are empowered – never tell them. Just give them power and reward them when they try to take more. Adopt the strategy of letting everyone in the company push at an open door. To achieve this, get out of the office and work for a day or two on the line, on the road, in the classroom, at the coal face. Find out where the beef is and give them the real power to sort it out.

To conclude, I think that culturally British industry is in pretty poor shape. Perhaps now it is time to stop for a minute or two and ask ourselves what is the purpose, the absolutely fundamental purpose, of an organisation? Surely, it must have something to do with creating economic, spiritual, intellectual and social wealth for people – workers on the inside and customers on the outside. But, as we've already discussed, the average company treats its customers appallingly, has a workforce driven by fear, with a management whose brains are atrophying and which operates for city institutions which seem to be only interested in making money in the shortest possible time for other institutions.

For our business leaders I have only one suggestion. Pour a very hot bath and a very large drink. Sit in one and consume slowly the other, and while you are doing this, think again.

THE CULTURAL DIMENSION
A Summary For Browsers

★ Passion.
★ Conviction.
★ Integrity.
★ Managers' actions are the most powerful agent for change in an organisation.
★ It's not about slogans and exhortations.
★ Culture is the fundamental essence of quality, Customer Care and business.
★ "If you ain't got it, you just can't fake it." (Crosby)
★ "It's just the way we do things round here." (ICL)
★ Culture of an organisation arises from signals people in the organisation receive.
★ Behaviour is the most powerful signal.
★ Behaviour, which impacts job security and job function, is the most powerful.
★ Perception and interpretation of behaviour is the key.
★ Delayering, downsizing and empowerment.
★ The real issue in business today is that of change; and to handle this, organisations need to be constantly learning and adapting.
★ Responsive evolution, not turbulent revolution.
★ We must re-think the role of our middle managers, not delayer them out of existence. Middle management should be the intellectual conduit for the organisation, the evolvers of our organisations not the defenders of the latest fads and fashions. They must become dedicated to enhancing tomorrow, not the status quo of today.

9

MAKING IT HAPPEN

To recap:

— Quality is about providing value to customers at appropriate cost.
— If the products or services you sell don't work, your cost base will rise to accommodate the handling of failures.
— To make products and services that work, the processes you use must be properly designed, developed, operated and controlled.
— Because you operate in a competitive environment, you must constantly improve your processes so that they yield better outputs, faster, cheaper.
— In a competitive environment you are either winning or losing, you can't stay still. To win you must be the best. Benchmarking is one way to find out how to be the best.
— In the real world, things will go wrong. When they do, you must put them right. But, you must put them right in such a way that the failure is corrected once and for all.
— To correct failures you must improve the processes that created them – correcting the process output is a short-term fix, which is too expensive to sustain long term.

— Failures can occur anywhere in an organisation, so you should invest in a formal correction system and training for all in its use.

The second dimension is the way in which customers are made to feel.

— Feelings and emotions are major drivers in the buying decisions of customers and are the major influences of a customer's loyalty.
— Loyal customers are cheaper to keep and will spend more with you.
— Customers talk to each other and they are free, willing and able to promote you or condemn you.
— Customer Care is the added dimension to quality. It is the human touch, the personal service, the empathy, and the responsiveness.
— Customer Care is the thousands of little every day things you can do to make the customer think, "Ooh! That was nice!"
— Your aim is to exceed the customer's expectations. Given how badly most companies treat most customers, it should not be too hard.

To bring all this about inside your organisation, you must achieve a change of culture.

— As a manager, it is fundamentally your responsibility to lead and drive the change.
— When everyone in the organisation is convinced that you and your management colleagues are really serious, then they will participate too.
— Only when this happens can you start to reap the rewards of all your hard work.

— You will need to reinforce constantly your commit-ment by words and actions.
— Remember that this is a long-term change, it will take years to make and you will never finish.
— As a manager, what you do is more important that what you say.
— Remember that when all is said and done, there's a lot more said than done!

It is unfortunate that there is no such thing as a recipe to make a change-receptive organisation. There can be no firm rules. Your organisation is different from any other and has features that are unique. Happily there are some guidelines.

The first stage is to recognise that you need to change. This is the "Why me? Why now?" phase. Unless you and your management colleagues are **absolutely convinced that you need to do something**, the best you will achieve will be a few weeks or months of Rah, Rah! This will inevitably be followed by the ignominious death of the programme, complete with an accompanying loss of management pride and integrity.

To help you plan the change in your organisation I have put together the following list as a "starter for ten". Discuss it with your colleagues. Extract from it those things you think could work for you. Generate your own ideas and add them to your list. Read the case study in Chapter 12 and decide if anything here is applicable to your circumstances. Talk to other companies to learn their lessons. Don't be afraid to call in expert help. But above all else – do something!

An Outline Action Plan

— Convince yourself that there is a real need in your organisation:
　　Survey your customers
　　Survey your colleagues
　　Survey your staff
　　Start to notice where you are incurring excessive costs
　　Look around and ask questions.
— Convince your management colleagues that the need is real and add their concerns to your own.
— As a management team positively decide to make change.
— Prepare a specific mission for this activity and modify your corporate mission if necessary.
— As a management team, actually select something to improve and improve it yourselves (both as a commitment action and as a process prototype).
— Form a management forum specifically to lead and oversee the programme, provide help to the organisation, develop enablers and review progress. (Depending upon the size of your organisation, you may need to create more than one of these.)
— Recognise that you may need help from external consultants. Think very hard about what you want them to achieve for you before you call them in. If you don't, you could spend a lot of money unnecessarily. If you do use consultants, try to get the best. For the same price, good consultants will achieve more for you in less time than poorer consultants for longer. (See Chapter 10.)
— Set top-level objectives and communicate them clearly, widely and in an imaginative and interesting way.

— Invest heavily in education and training for everyone to help you establish a common vision and a common language.

— Use the best communicators within your management team as instructors.

— During the training explain why the need for change. Why does the organisation need to change? Why does each work-group need to change? Why must individuals change? Etc. What are the benefits of change – to the customers, suppliers, organisation, work-groups, individuals, etc?

— Also in the training, launch your new mission and explain any modifications to the corporate mission. Also demonstrate that you are serious by showing everyone that something has already been improved.

— Try and create a few highly paid, senior, influential champions for the cause. Help and encourage the

Positively expected to rock the boat.

champions to become expert in the subject. Allow them to visit other companies, attend conferences, walk and talk freely inside your organisation, have ready access to the top team.

— Insist that your champions be disobedient, outspoken, vociferous enthusiasts who are not merely allowed to, but positively expected to, rock the corporate boat.

— Design a reporting system for problems and invest resources and senior staff to ensure that they are solved.

— Design a system for recognising achievements and support for the new culture. Ensure that this system is absolutely fair; anyone can make a recognition to anyone with rewards not of cash or expensive gifts, but instead creative, sincere, personal and grateful – public thanks.

— Aim to double the personal contact of all managers with all staff inside the organisation.

— Aim to double the amount of direct customer contact made by your organisation (managers and staff).

— For every work-group in the organisation, find out what causes staff the most irritation – and actively participate in helping them to sort it out. Then, tell them to do it again themselves for the next most unsatisfactory feature of the group's activities and report back.

— Recognise that, "If we are proud of ourselves, the place will be evidence of our pride." Conduct a "make the place look nice" blitz and then introduce a process to make sure that it stays that way.

— Identify the key business processes in the organisation and document them.

— Initiate a review of these business processes to identify major weaknesses or improvement opportunities.

— Develop a system whereby everyone knows what is going on.
— Follow-up the initial training with further training, and further training.
— Every year, take a deep breath and take a long hard look at your progress and then reaffirm the needs and your commitment and then review all the systems to ensure that they are still OK.
— Always remember Winston Churchill's words, "Never, never, never quit!"
— . . . And most importantly of all – HAVE FUN!

10

CONSULTING CONSULTANTS

Assuming that, as a management team, you have decided that you really do need to make a change, the next stage is to start some serious thinking about what, why, how, when, where, etc. You need to develop a mission, strategy and plans. Next, you will need to create and build your support systems (for example: education, recognition and corrective action). Then comes control and monitoring systems and then cyclic implementation. At any of these stages you may feel that you need help from external consultants.

Consultants are not cheap (I should know, I am one) and so it is essential that you get the best value you can from them. To help you do this; the following notes tell you a bit about these people.

Firstly, we need to understand what a consultant is. We need a definition. Like the definition of quality, there are a number of widely used ones. Here are three.

The Institute of Management Consultancy defines a consultant as:

"An independent and qualified person who provides a professional service to clients by:
— Identifying and investigating problems

- Formulating recommendations for action by investigation and analysis, with due regard for broader management and business implications
- Discussing and agreeing with the client the most appropriate course of action
- Providing assistance where required by the client to implement the recommendations made."

Another respected definition is:

"The rendering of independent advice and assistance about management issues. This typically includes:
- Identifying and investigating problems and/or opportunities
- Recommending appropriate action
- Helping to implement recommendations."

These are the types of formal definitions which consultants like you to know about. The third definition, while widely used inside the industry, is one that few consultants tell clients about – even if this is the one they actually use themselves!

"A Management Consultant, more often than not, is someone brought in to find out what has gone wrong by the people who made it go wrong, in the comfortable belief that s/he will not bite off the hand that feeds him/her by placing the blame where it belongs."

The point about these definitions is that to get the best value from consultants requires that you have a very clear idea about what you want – before you call them in.

Any programme of change you wish to make happen in your business belongs to you – not a consultant. Sure, a minority of sharp consultants will be only too happy to adopt ownership of your partially thought-out programme and then design something that meets your all-too-vague brief. They will be delighted to do this, in many cases, because they will simply trot out the solution that they developed for a previous client. They will take a long time over it and charge you fees accordingly, and you will end up with something that no one owns. So, after the consultant leaves, you will blame every problem on him and he will account for the failure of your organisation not running things properly.

The golden rule with consultants is to be specific about what you want.

Hang on a minute. That's a rule. Throughout the book I have been saying that there are no rules.

This "rule" is no exception. Yes, you should be specific in briefing a consultant but your requirements should be flexible enough for you to modify your plans to accommodate any good ideas the consultant may have. The point is that *you* decide which ideas are good – not the consultant. Never fall into the trap of relinquishing ownership of the programme.

To help you be precise, it is helpful to recognise that a consultant operates in four general roles. By thinking about the role that you want the consultant to fill, you will be able to scope the assignment more effectively. The roles are show in the box opposite.

The majority of good professional consultants much prefer to work under specific terms of reference and will encourage you to be precise. In such conditions the consultant can work to ensure that s/he is really delivering high value and is securing your loyalty. His business, after all, is just as much driven by a need for continuous improvement, Customer Care and business excellence as yours is.

He may even go so far as to offer you consultancy to

Facilitator:	"Let me help you to resolve your situation for yourself."
Solver:	"Although I do not have an answer, I do have skills which will enable me to reach a solution for you."
Advisor:	"I have come across this situation before, this is what you could/should do."
Executive:	"My experience is best used in this situation by my taking a line management role in your organisation."

define the requirements for a consultant. This is not usually a cheap trick to earn a few more days of fees; it is good process management to ensure clear and agreed requirements.

However, consultancy is an unregulated industry and so some are better than others. You being specific will help you judge the likely value you are being offered.

A good consultant will want to work with you, not for you. He will want to form a long lasting relationship and so will stay in touch. He will want to learn your business, to enable him to serve you better. He will want to win your trust and confidence, to enable him to add value to your ideas. He will want access to your people, because he knows that staff often tell consultants things they wouldn't tell managers; he can then offer higher value advice.

A good consultant may (or may not) charge a relatively high fee per day, but he will always strive to ensure that: his fee-earning days deliver value, and that he only earns fees when there is need for him to do so.

Most consultants are professional, but there are some sharks amongst them. Those with a ready-made recipe should set your antennae trembling. As should those who know all the answers, or talk "consulting-speak", or appear to relish revolution.

Keep alert and keep specific, and you should be able to sort the wheat from the chaff.

11

TRAINING YOUR TRAINERS

"I hear and I forget, I see and I remember, I do and I understand."

As we have seen, one of the most vital things to do when managing change is the provision of supporting training and education for everyone involved. They will need to know what your visions, values, missions, objectives, strategies and plans are, as well as the rationale behind them. They will need to understand and buy-in to their role and become effective in managing the change within their own processes. They will probably therefore need to develop process engineering skills, quality management and control skills, problem solving skills. All your managers and staff will need to be educated in the concepts and principles surrounding the change you wish to effect. There simply is no short cut. Education and training is the foundation upon which everything else is based. Like change itself, education and training is an on-going commitment to your people. It is also the on-going catalyst of cultural development.

Much of this is not training in the conventional sense. Unlike most training the transfer of knowledge or skills forms only a minor part. The fundamental role of this type of training is to initiate and/or support a change of attitude. For this training and education to support change in your organisation it must be designed to meet your specific needs and be targeted at your people and their culture. Even if you have a vast training budget (and I know very few who do), it would be foolish to expect off-the-shelf courses purchased from training suppliers to meet all your requirements. This is one management issue which cannot be solved by simply throwing money at it. Of course specialist external trainers may give you a very sound basis upon which to build and, as such, provide high value, but even if you base your training upon their ideas you will need to (and should anyway) develop and deliver much of the training yourselves.

Many organisations have a Personnel function that "owns" training. In most cases this means that Personnel staff purchase and administer the delivery of standard training courses by outside agencies. Very few Personnel staff are trained trainers, very few have experience in education, even fewer have experience of change management and, because of the role that they perform, few of them really have a feel for the culture and attitudes of managers and staff in operating units. For these reasons, I would suggest that, for most organisations, entrusting the Personnel department with this training and education would be to take a considerable risk. Of course I am generalising, some Personnel/training departments employ real experts in the field of people development. If you do employ such talent, of course you must use it. But even in this case, I would recommend that you do not give them management control of this training.

I strongly recommend that you establish a team of senior managers, taken in only small part from Headquarters and predominantly from line units, to develop and maintain an education and training strategy and become your cadre of

teachers. Each of these managers should,
selected on the basis of the following criteri
listed in order of importance:

— Individual credibility with managers and s   ne
  organisation
— A track record of making things happen
— General enthusiasm for the subject and for your
  organisation
— Being an independent spirit
— A track record of taking risks
— Verbal communication skills.

These managers are not going to be easy to release from their
normal jobs. So, the temptation will be great to select other
managers in their place. Don't do it! Once these lesser managers find themselves in front of their own staff, their weaknesses will be exposed for all to see. Standing up in front of
any audience is tough; but standing up in front of an in-house
audience often feels like being in the company of a team of
voyeuristic radiologists – they undress you down to the
bones! This is one job that really does need your best people.

By selecting your teacher/managers with extreme care
you will create a strong team who know your business and
who are ideally placed to identify the issues which need to
be addressed. As this team comprises senior credible people, they will have relatively easy access to the top team to
learn of their concerns. As the team comprises enthusiasts,
they will get things done. As they are good communicators
they will demonstrate management commitment at every
stage. This cadre of teachers is likely to be your source of
vociferous enthusiasts, mentioned in Chapter 9, who will
be encouraged to rock the boat. They will identify the need
for further teachers, select them and train them. You can

They undress you down to the bones.

be sure that they will be every bit as selective as you will –
it's their personal credibility that is on the line.

The remainder of this chapter is written especially with
these teachers in mind, but almost all of it applies to any
manager giving any presentation to anyone.

It's not the Teacher's Job to Teach

Imparting information, knowledge or skill to others is
probably the most important and rewarding achievement
of our species. By doing so you are directly adding value to
the lives of others. Parents do it to children and call it love
and adults do it to their ageing parents and call it caring.
Cultural and social revolutions have occurred as a result
of it and martyrs have died for it. Some presenters are
poorly rewarded for their vocation while others have been

venerated, applauded and been made obscencly rich.

Every one of us has done it and had it done to us. Sometimes it has been done well while at others it has not. Can we learn from this and discover some of the features of success and failure? Can we learn about learning and can notes such as these teach about teaching? I hope so for that is my intent.

These guidelines are actually generic and apply to any factual presentation. I have coined the term "teaching" to describe any presentation of information to others, which has the purpose of providing them with skill or knowledge.

The base line for these notes, and for every single effective teacher of anything, I like to describe as my First Principle of Education: *It Is Not The Teacher's Job To Teach. It Is The Teacher's Job To Get The Student To Learn.*

But is this the whole story? I think not. I would suggest that the principle, "Teachers don't teach but instead get students to learn," is necessary, but not sufficient. I believe that really good teachers have a second driving aim. And that is, that the teacher learns about his own material from his student. At first this sounds odd, but the reasoning is simple. Everyone is unique. Therefore, everyone learns in a unique way. Therefore, each learner manipulates the information presented to him uniquely. So, if a teacher concentrates all his energy to understanding how the student is manipulating the information presented, the teacher must inevitably gain further insight into his material. The teacher has, in effect, learned his material from the student. The teacher cannot achieve this aim unless he has achieved *both* the student's learning, and a comprehension of the student's learning processes.

So, my First Principle of Education reads:

"It must be the aim of any teacher that the student learns, not that he teaches."

And, my Second Principle reads:

> *"It is the ultimate aim of a competent teacher that s/he secures new insight into his material from his student."*

These principles are more than an interesting academic debate or a clever play on words. They force the realisation that when you are in the role of presenter, trainer or coach you must dedicate *all* of your energy externally, not internally. Despite my discussing the feelings of the presenter later in these notes, the only feelings that really matter are those of the students. Taking these principles into account will help you give a reasonable presentation. If you fail to become student focused, you can polish your material until the shine is dazzling, and your presentations will fail – without fail.

Profile of Adult Students/Audiences
Teaching adults is not the same as teaching children. Adults are both physically and mentally different and these differences must be appreciated if you are to develop an effective presentation strategy. The following profile of adult learners highlights some of these important characteristics.

Adults are people who:

— Have practical experience and knowledge.
— Relate what you say to that which they already know.
— Learn by doing.
— Have ideas of their own and are willing (usually) to share them.
— Are busy and have a lot on their minds (work, home, car . . .).
— Have established attitudes and values.
— Can change (sometimes willingly, sometimes less so).
— Respond to reinforcement.

— Need to be recognised.
— Are physically large (disproportionate mass to seated surface area).

Approach

Adults display a number of characteristics which you must accommodate in your teaching event if it is to be effective. Adults occupy a "real world" of practical issues and have things on their mind; your presentation must, therefore, motivate as well as inform. This is a requirement on both the design of the event and on the delivery of it. The following notes on motivation and style apply equally both to the design phase and the delivery phase of your presentation. For example, adults are physically large (disproportionate mass to seated surface area), your design must therefore ensure that the event contains break points, but as the deliverer you also have a role. Your display of energy will offset their physical passivity and therefore sustain a higher level of attention for longer.

Motivation

Adults like learning, but the fact that they are busy and have other things on their minds makes learning more difficult. To succeed, you must motivate your audience to suspend these other issues and focus on your material. Consider:

What's in it for ME	**WIFM**	the individual listener/student.
What's in it for US	**WIFU**	the student's peer group.
What's in it for YOU	**WIFY**	the presenter.
What's in it for THEM	**WIFT**	outside bodies – society, the world, the organisation, and so on.

Generally, the degree of motivation diminishes from the first to the last. As a presenter, it is your job to ensure that the audience is, and continues to be, motivated. Pepper your presentation with WIFMs to achieve this.

Style Strategies
WIFMs are only one way in which a positive learning environment is created. (Remember that this is a function of both the event design and the event dynamics.) The style of the event and its presenter also has a significant effect. Consider:

Concept	vs.	Rote
Feedback	vs.	Vacuum
Active	vs.	Passive
Positive	vs.	Neutral

Clearly, there will be exceptions, but those on the left should usually be your guide.

"Rote" is a list of facts; "Concept" is the principle behind the fact. As adults relate new information to that which they already know, "teaching by concept" is almost invariably a more successful (and popular) strategy than "teaching by rote".

"Vacuum" is where an audience merely receives information; "Feedback" is where they question, discuss and are similarly involved. Remember that adults relate what you say to that which they already know, so "vacuum" is less likely to be a successful strategy.

"Active" and "Passive" relate to the fact that adults generally learn by doing. An "active" strategy (e.g. a workshop investigating real issues) is likely to sustain audience interest for an extended period and help them to retain the messages.

"Positive" and "Neutral" relate to the presenter's

attitude to his audience and the matter being presented. A "positive" approach enables you to enthuse your audience and so change their views and to enthuse yourself – making you more likely to provide reinforcement and recognition.

Hence:

Explain why something is so, not merely that it is so; get your audience to discover rather than just being told; if you don't care about your subject the audience definitely won't.

Preparing Your Presentation

I estimate that at least 15 hours of preparation are required for each hour standing up and "doing it". (This assumes that you do NOT need to research facts first.) The most common reaction to this assertion is "Rubbish – it can't take that long"! Please believe me, it does! Some professional presenters actually assert that it takes considerably longer than this. The point is simple and vital. *The need for planned, careful preparation cannot be over emphasised.*

Event Aims and Objectives

All presentations require preparation. The first and most valuable phase of this preparation is determining the Aims and Objectives of the event.

An Aim is a statement of that which the event will provide. Objectives, in this context, are statements, which describe what each of your audience will be able to do as a result of the event. For example:

AIM

This event will provide an audience of technical staff and managers with an introduction to the preparation, mechanics, and dynamics of a teaching presentation.

OBJECTIVES

At the end each member of the audience will be able to:

— Differentiate between child and adult learners
— Explain the four teaching levels of motivation
— Explain the four stylistic strategies.

When writing Objectives you will find it most helpful to use "Active" verbs. Verbs, which describe something tangible, are so much easier to test. If you set a tangible objective, then you can check that your event is effective by testing. If your objective was vague, you are unlikely ever to be able to find out how effective you were.

Good verbs include:

analyse	*arrange*	*avoid*	*build*
calculate	*conduct*	*construct*	*convince*
create	*describe*	*design*	*eliminate*
explain	*express*	*function as*	*identify*
increase	*justify*	*list*	*maintain*
measure	*motivate*	*negotiate*	*obtain*
perform	*produce*	*promote*	*provide*
reduce	*save*	*simplify*	*test*
use	*write*		

Avoid verbs such as:

appreciate	*be aware of*	*believe*	*comprehend*
consider	*feel*	*fully appreciate*	*know*
learn	*relate to*	*think*	*understand*

In addition to "individual objectives", other objectives may need to be specified, e.g. organisation objectives – "at the end of the event, to [dept. A], the organisation will be able to . . . [i.e. exploit this opportunity] and will demonstrate this by . . ."

The articulation of the event objectives is the single most helpful activity in event design and development, as from it everything else follows. An event which is trying to do the right things for the right people, but which is poorly structured or presented will have a higher level of overall effectiveness than one which is presented brilliantly, structured superbly but is teaching the wrong thing.

When developing an event you should write down these objectives, as they will be referred to repeatedly. You should scope each objective statement and have indicators of success for each – ask yourself "What constitutes success here and how will I know that I have achieved it?"

The teaching and examination of trainee drivers in Britain contains many examples of such objectives, e.g. the "Three point turn" [sic]. The student objective is that he:

Demonstrates the ability to turn the car around using both forward and reverse gears in a controlled and safe fashion.

Note: He is not required to "do it in three"! But the objective states that it must be controlled, so if he hits the kerb he's failed. The instructor, driving examiner and the student are all working to the same set of objectives; they all know what is expected of them and of each other. Given the staggering complexity and risk associated with the management in real time of a high velocity missile operating in the same domain as thousands of other similar missiles, it is remarkable that anyone learns to drive at all. The fact that most of us have done so without undue stress and in only a few weeks or months demonstrates the effectiveness of a well conducted teaching event. It also serves to demonstrate the outstanding value of well articulated objectives; any errors, ambiguities or omissions would make learning to drive a (literally) grave occasion (!).

Scoping the Audience

This is another phase in sound preparation. Knowing some of the answers to the following questions will help you get the "pitch right". It will also help you decide how you will structure the presentation.

— What do they already know?
— What do they want to know?
— What do they need to know?
— Why do they need to know?
— What is their attitude to the presentation going to be?

Session Content

Any event of longer than about an hour will need to be broken down into sessions, each one being a digestible "chunk". The criteria for deciding the sessions are based upon the ease of learning not the ease of presentation.

Having decided the event aims and objectives and related these to the audience, you need to consider each session.

— What are the session objectives (i.e. what will they be able to do)? The answer to this will help you to define meaningful boundaries for the session.
— What can they do at the start of the session (given previous sessions)? The answer to this will help you "pitch" your presentation and decide your recap points.
— Why can't they do this now? The answer to this will greatly help define the session content.
— What are they likely to get wrong in attempting to practise this objective? The answer to this will help you to decide the Key Points.

Session Structure

Having defined the event aim and objectives, and having related this to your audience and having now defined the content of each session based upon a set of session objectives you can now decide the structure of your presentation to best effect. In most cases the structure should be presented to your audience "up front" as this helps them "tune in" and stops them getting lost.

Consider a structure along the following lines:

EVENT

SESSION 1

Administration
Start times, break times, smoking rules, refreshments, etc.

Introduction
Motivate, objectives of session, content for next hour.

Topic A
Introduction, content, summary, test understanding, link to next topic.

Topic B
Introduction, content, summary, test understanding, recap content within context of previous topic/s.

Summary
Restate objectives, key headings, take questions, actions.

Link To Session 2

SESSION 2

Introduction – as above

and so on.

PRESENTATION TECHNIQUES

Managing the Environment

Before you start, you need to ensure that the environment is conducive to your delivery. Doing so will not motivate your audience, but failure to do so will de-motivate them.

— Student comfort?
— Your comfort?
— Interruptions?
— Noise and distractions?
— Start and end times?
— How will they get there?
— Food/drink?
— Comfort breaks?

Understanding You

As a presenter you are the focus of attention. This has a number of repercussions:

— You will be nervous.
— It's an ego trip.
— You are responsible to make the subject "live".
— You know more about it than the audience (else why are they wasting your and THEIR time?).
— Approximately 95% of your little glitches and blunders (including the uncontrollable jitters) will not be observed by the audience.
— All audiences are on your side – they want you to do well as much as you do (they've got to sit through it after all) – do you want your teachers to fail?

The most important thing to be when on your toes is . . .

YOURSELF. By all means study techniques and the tricks of the trade but if it isn't YOU then don't do it.

With Conviction

Effective delivery depends to a huge extent upon the conviction you communicate. This requires two major abilities – *Showing Confidence* and *Showing Enthusiasm*.

Showing confidence doesn't mean being confident; it means looking confident. Even the most expert presenter will feel nervous no matter how practised. If you don't feel jittery you're almost certain to do a lousy job.

The critical time for showing confidence is in the first few minutes, for it is then that you create your first impression (and you won't ever get a second chance). The bad news is that it is in the first few minutes that you feel least confident – once you are into your stride the

How will you remove your jacket?

butterflies will tend to go. So what should you do to ensure that you get off to a good start?

Simply, the answer is to plan, prepare and rehearse, and for these first few minutes do so in minute detail. Plan and practise your walk-on – this isn't being a prima donna it is being a professional. Where will you come from? Where will you walk to? What precisely will be your first action? How (or) will you remove your jacket? You are establishing yourself as the centre of attention. Are you positioned out in the open or are you hiding behind a desk or podium? What will you wear? Are your shoes clean? Remember it is the first few seconds that set the tone for the entire event in the minds of the audience – be positive. "Unaccustomed as I am to public speaking" is an excuse used by amateurs who shouldn't be speaking at all!

Showing enthusiasm was discussed in the section on style strategy. But how does one go about doing it?

Remember that your enthusiasm is that which commands attention. Therefore to show enthusiasm you must be larger than life. To do this you must stimulate both the ears and the eyes of the audience.

You will know from your rehearsals how loudly you need to speak to be heard in the room. What you must then do is set your volume control about 10% higher than this. Having done so, you will still have enough vocal power left to "hit them loud" for emphasis and have enough acoustic scope to reduce the volume for effect and still be clearly heard.

Non-verbal communication also transmits enthusiasm or a lack of it. What you wear, how you stand, how and when you walk about the room, and how and when you use your hands all have an effect. So, to summarise **BE YOURSELF – BUT MAGNIFIED.**

But remember, remember, remember it's them that really matter, not you. Thinking about them and how they are feeling is the key factor in showing confidence and enthusiasm.

Start with a bang!

Delivery – Hints and Tips
— Start with a bang!
— Keep conclusions short and simple. And put in mini-conclusions frequently – it tells them they've got somewhere.
— Examples should be frequent, simple and non-contentious.
— *Always* think about the audience – your objective is that they learn not that you teach.

— Maintain eye contact.
— Vary the speed of delivery.
— Avoid misuse of hands – use them for emphasis not conducting your words.
— Use pauses.
— When asking questions don't be frightened of silence – they will answer. (Presenters often find silence "deafening" and jump in too soon. This has the effect of *vacuum* (see page 154), and worse, telling the group "It's OK not to think".)
— Watch out for "those endearing little habits" (the habitual turn of phrase, e.g. "you know what I mean" or the habitual behaviour, e.g. the hair flick every couple of minutes) so loved by the kids, they're bound to irritate someone.
— Talk from notes not a script.
— Do not learn by heart your presentation – one question and you'll be all over the place. The only exception to this rule is in the theatre when you are talking at people rather than to them (e.g. large conference, talking at a camera, etc.).
— Keep your head up when you speak, stand up straight, don't mumble, gabble or shout. (Remember the old elocution classes: Miss Prim talked about "Projection".)
— Above all else PREPARE and REHEARSE.

Handling Questions

Many inexperienced presenters dread questions, failing to realise how helpful they are. A question confirms that you were being listened to and provides you with real feedback about how well you were meeting your overall objective – "that they learn". Questions enable you to deal with misunderstandings quickly, they help you judge the attitude of your audience to the material you are presenting and often they open-up an area for discussion that is very valuable, but not actually covered by your well honed script.

As with almost everything else in the presentation business, handling questions is about preparation. What are the ten questions you would least like to be asked? Now prepare answers to each, following these five steps:

Listen
Let them finish without interruption if possible, only intervene if you are faced with a rambler.

Pause For Thought
At least three full seconds. This silence allows you to consider carefully the question *and* creates a definite break in which you regain control.

Test Understanding
Check that everyone in the group has heard the question and check that you have understood it.

Answer The Question
Clearly and briefly to the whole group (to retain attention), avoiding going off on a new track. If you don't know the answer, say so and either tell the questioner where to find the answer or commit to get an answer.

Check That You've Answered The Question
Ask, "Does that cover your question?", and listen for the response; it may be a supplementary question in which case go back to the start of the process again.

Remember to tell the audience, up-front, when you will deal with questions. In general, dealing with them as they arise is best for small groups, but set question times are better for large conference groups.

Visual Aids

Please, please, please remember that visual *aids* are precisely that. More presentations than a few die because they are being used as a crutch. The purpose of a visual is to reinforce the spoken word. Ask yourself, "How does this visual aid enhance what I am saying?" As an aside, a picture paints a thousand words.

Here are a few specific guidelines:

— Keep slides simple.
  (Rule of Seven: maximum of seven lines; maximum of seven words per line.)
— Use colour sensibly.
  (Rule of Three: maximum of three per slide – plus black.)
— Unless you are very skilled don't hand-write acetates.
— When writing flip charts, draw faint straight lines with yellow chalk.
  (Only you will see it.)
— When writing on a white/black board, use brief notes not text.
  (Aim to write less than four words.)
— Use a variety of visuals.
  (Overhead projector, flip chart, white-board, video, models, etc.)
— Talk to the audience not the visual aid.
— Avoid pointers, pencils etc.
  (Most people fiddle with them and it's distracting to the audience.)
— Avoid "gradual reveal" on a slide.
  (Nobody listens; they are all speculating about the hidden bit.)
— Be very cautious about multi-layer slides.
  (It's so easy to put it together in the wrong order.)

— In general, do not move away from the slide. Though there are occasions when it can be effective to do so, the usual result is that the audience becomes distracted because it doesn't know whether to look at you, or at the slide.
— Always check that everyone can see the visuals. (Sight lines.)
— What will you do if the bulb/fuse/projector fails midstream?
— With all visual aids, but especially models and demonstration pieces, never forget the old adage of the theatre that inanimate objects are out to get you. Like the theatre, two things protect you – simplicity and practice.

Why Much Training Doesn't Work
Much training in British organisations today is centred on the formal training course. Managers frequently think that by sending their staff on a course, their training needs will be addressed. When, later, they discover that not all training needs have been satisfied, they blame the course and the trainer, not realising that it is themselves who are to blame for the failure. Training which centres around attendance on courses often tends to be focused upon the development of isolated skills for an individual. In most cases, what is actually required is training and education which is focused upon the development of skills which will be applied within a team context back at the work-place. It is the failure to integrate the training and education back into the business which accounts for much of the waste of organisations' training budgets and for the apparent inability of organisations to manage cultural change.

It is vital that companies adopt a structured approach to

the training experience. But too many managers see attendance on a training course as an end in itself. To be effective, a course needs to be the middle segment of a three-phase process:

—   Preparation
—   The Course Itself
—   Follow-up and Application.

Preparation starts with the delegate and the manager, together, articulating why s/he is attending and what end result is desired. This is followed by the determination of how this end result will be applied back on the job, along with an assessment of the benefits of this application to both the individual and to the organisation. Only after this work has been done is the delegate motivated to learn and focused towards applying the learning for personal and business benefit. Sadly, in too many cases, this work is not done. This is why most trainers, at the beginning of most courses, spend time exploring these questions with the delegates. Of course it is too late to be asking, "What are you doing here?" at the start of the course. The trainer is making a brave attempt to cover a management failing, but in fact is really doing little more than wasting the first hour or so of the course. Not only is the work being done at the wrong time, but the trainer should not be doing it at all. Few trainers have sufficient prior knowledge of the delegates or their business to be able to lead the discussions effectively.

The loss of training effectiveness caused by a failure to prepare is considerable; but the loss caused by a failure to follow-up is even worse.

Follow-up is the process whereby what has been learned is retained and then applied back into the day-job. Given that the knowledge and skills presented on the course represent 100%, we can expect delegates to take away about 75%.

The 25% loss is normal and is built-in to any well-designed and delivered course. All training comprises three sets of information:

— Must Knows
— Should Knows
— Could Knows.

A competent trainer ensures that *all* delegates have secured *all* the "Must Knows" and most of the "Should Knows". The "Could Knows" are reinforcing and so few need to be retained. A 70%-80% capture of the course material by the delegate is consistent with a successful course – the skills and/or knowledge having been effectively transferred.

Follow-up ensures retention and application of this 70%-80%, and, if done really well, enables the delegate to improve even on this figure.

Follow-up should start within a week of completing the course. At this time, the delegate should spend a short period reviewing the course content. For a course of 1-2 days, fifteen minutes of focused attention is usually sufficient. A failure to do this greatly reduces retention typically to 50%-60%. The next phase of follow-up is Application. This involves reviewing the preparation phase in which application of the training was planned and ensuring that the training is integrated into the workplace. Performing this task with care actually raises retention, but a failure to do so reduces it further – typically to the point where only about 25% of what was taught is retained. Within six months, without follow-up, the retention is usually considerably less than 10%. So, if the cost of sending a delegate on a course was £200 in fees, £200 in accommodation and £1,000 in lost opportunity costs (arising from the delegate not doing the day job), you have spent a total of £1,400. If retention is less than 10% and there is no application of the training, the delegate has a notional benefit from the training of £20 recovered from the course fee. And you and the business have a benefit of zero! If, on the other hand, preparation has been done effectively (supported by line management), and follow-up and application have been done well, the benefit could massively exceed 100%. The delegate will have developed extensions of the training, shared the skills and knowledge with colleagues and secured business advantages from the application.

The additional costs of preparation and follow-up are trivial. All that is needed is a few minutes planning before the course, a few minutes application planning soon after it, and a short period of revision a month or two later. Surely no delegate and no company can afford to ignore preparation and follow-up? But tragically, in many companies they do!

TRAINING YOUR TRAINERS
A Summary For Browsers

Profile of an Adult Audience
★ Adults have experience and a point of view, and are busy.
★ "Understand them before you start."

Teaching Approach
★ Concepts.
★ Feedback.

★ Active.
★ Positive.
★ Motivation – "What's in it for me."
★ "Tune into their needs in the planning phase."

Preparation
★ Aims and Objectives *most* important.
★ Who is audience?
★ Sessions.
★ Structure
    First I tells 'em what I'll tell 'em,
    Then I tell 'em,
    Then I tell 'em what I've told 'em.
★ "The most vital phase of the lot. Invest time, effort and care on it."

Presentation Techniques
★ Environment.
★ Everyone has butterflies.
★ Be enthusiastic.
★ Watch for irritating habits.
★ Listen to the students.
★ Work from notes.
★ Rehearsals (!)
★ "Just be yourself – magnified."

Visual Aids
★ Keep them simple.

Why Most Training Doesn't Work
★ Preparation.
    Why attend?
    What benefits?
    Expected changes?

★ Follow-up.
   Revision.
   Application.
   Retention.

12

DOES IT WORK IN PRACTICE?

A DECADE-LONG CASE STUDY: A PROGRAMME OF BUSINESS AND CULTURAL CHANGE IN "ICL HIGH PERFORMANCE TECHNOLOGY"

Background

ICL plc is Europe's premier computer and information technology supplier that, in November 1990, became an autonomous company within the Fujitsu group of companies. During the period of this case study (1985-1995/6), ICL operated in over 85 countries, employed approximately 25,000 people and had an annual turnover of around £2 billion.

"High Performance Technology" is the name I have used for ICL's research and development group responsible for the design, development and integration of large, high performance computer systems. In fact, over the decade, this organisation has evolved, been re-branded and repositioned within the parent corporation many times. For reasons of simplicity and brevity I have used throughout the brand name that was extant at the end of the period and have abbreviated this to "HPT". In reality, at the start of the case study it was an operating (R&D cost centre) division of ICL called "Mainframe Systems Division" which later became "Corporate Systems Division". By the mid 1990s, ICL created an organisation called "High Performance Systems" (HPS) as an autonomous business unit within the ICL Group (accountable for both costs and revenues). Within this business unit, the R&D group became known as "High Performance Technology."

HPT (and its forebears) has been sited at West Gorton in Manchester, since before the Second World War and has been directly involved in the development of computers from the earliest days of the technology. Its function throughout its existence has been the research, development and bringing to market of large general purpose data processing technology and products, including mainframe computers and high-speed, high-volume peripherals. These products are typically used by large organisations to support key corporate business processes and manage mission critical data. Evolving customer demand has necessitated the continuous development and innovative engineering of advanced technology to yield ever-greater capacity and speed with higher standards of reliability and security at a reducing cost of ownership.

In the period of this study, HPT employed approximately 1,000 full-time staff. It had over 25% of the UK large computer systems market and an installed worldwide base in excess of 1,800 systems, predominantly in the financial services, local and central government, public utilities and retail market sectors.

In 1982 the organisation first became accredited to an internationally recognised quality management system – MOD standard 05-21.

1985
Many customer surveys, meetings, and telephone contacts asked, "How are we doing?" Feedback says that ICL has a

poor reputation, its targets are too low, and ICL is an introspective company that puts quality in as an afterthought. Customers say that they want "less talk and more action" from ICL.

At the same time ICL calculates how much mistakes cost. This analysis shows that 20% of all resources are spent in re-work, correction and managing problems.

The ICL Main Board set four key objectives:

—   Change the way we think about quality
—   Establish a common language
—   Establish a continuous process for quality improvement
—   Train everybody.

The ICL Main Board writes the ICL Quality policy:

"We will provide competitive systems, products and services which fully meet our internal and external customers' requirements first time, on time, and every time."

HPT wins Queen's Award for Technical Achievement for Series 39 CAFS-ISP.

1986

The HPT Managing Director attends a two-and-a-half-day course describing the role of the executive in quality management.

Eighty-one of HPT's top managers attend a four-day course that explains the manager's role and gives them time to plan how the Quality Improvement Process will be introduced. (Courses supplied by Philip Crosby Associates.)

The HPT Managing Director establishes the Quality Steering Group (8 July) to lead and oversee the drive for quality improvement within HPT. Groups of senior managers establish Quality Improvement Teams to plan and develop the tools for the implementation of quality improvement.

The systems software development group starts to focus on customer complaints (bug reports) and customer dissatisfaction. A pilot improvement programme is run which halves the backlog of outstanding complaints in five weeks (from approximately 1,000 down to 500).

1987

On 13 January, teams of senior managers start delivery of a series of 20-hour duration training courses to all managers and staff in HPT (including all members of the board, and the MD himself).

ICL Main Board Directors receive a one-day overview of this training and commit to attend the full course.

A two-hour follow-up module is developed and is delivered by all line managers to their teams a few months after completing the 20-hour initial training course.

The HPT Managing Director personally leads a programme to improve "Support and Bug Fixing" processes. By year-end the backlog of software problem reports had been reduced from over 1,200 to approximately 200.

VME (ICL's mainframe computer operating system) demonstrates a 30-fold reliability improvement over the year.

Customer critical situations reduced from an average of 30 to an average of 5 active at any one time.

A formal Corrective Action system is launched in all areas. This provides a mechanism for identifying process problems and managing improvements.

One Corrective Action is taken by an administrator who saves £30,000 per year by improving the control of training course cancellations.

A one-day Total Quality Management course for customers/suppliers/collaborators is developed and delivered to executives from major customer organisations so that they can benefit from the Division's experiences thus far.

HPT invests in the development of the Core Technical Training Programme. This is an integrated education and training programme designed for the whole of ICL's technical community, covering such areas as quality, design, engineering, business, and technology trends. The structure of the programme provides each member of technical staff with a complete programme of education and training throughout his/her entire career, encompassing such features as Chartered Engineer accreditation, academic research study, extensive business and technology awareness and the development of technical, managerial, commercial and personal skills.

At the start of the year the overall reliability of ICL's small/medium-sized mainframe computers averaged 20 breaks per year per system. (See following notes – 1989.)

1988

All the 20-hour training courses completed on 28 May (1,500 people trained) – everyone in HPT. Delivery of the follow-up training by line managers continues.

ICL wins The National Training Award for quality training.

Quality Management Teams are established to drive the implementation of quality improvements within work-groups. Also a number of ad hoc steering teams are formed to provide specific enablers (e.g. Corrective

Action, Recognition, Awareness, Cost of Quality).

The HPT computer services organisation reviews and improves the scheduling of the systems so that more efficient use is made of the machines and the rate of change of development systems is optimised. This saves an estimated £22,000 per week.

HPT wins Queen's Award for technical achievement for optical fibre technology.

1989
All staff complete follow-up training. Further follow-up training is developed.

ICL wins second National Training Award for the Core Technical Programme.

HPT holds a major 3-day event involving all staff and hosting over 5,000 visitors, including families, customers, suppliers and community representatives (in October) to celebrate a change of attitude to quality, a recognition of achievements so far, and a re-commitment to continuing the drive for improvement. At the event, HPT is awarded its BS5750/ISO9001 certificate (achieved at first attempt). HPT's target to reduce its total costs of failure by 10% over the year is exceeded by nearly three times. Seventy-five per cent of all customer small/medium mainframe computer systems had no service interruptions at all within the first quarter of the year – the improvement trend continued.

An HPT programme of "Joint Quality Management Teams" is designed and launched in which HPT managers and customer managers work together, combining the resources of both organisations, to identify and implement improvements for joint benefit. Early customers include Her Majesty's Stationery Office, British Telecom, Britannia Building Society and the Inland Revenue.

The HPT director responsible for operating systems development is presented with a Gold Excellence award in Switzerland for being a personal role model and inspirational leader. His nomination was made by his own staff.

Mainframe manufacturing factory wins Britain's Best Factory award.

1990

Mainframe manufacturing factory wins British Quality Award from the British Quality Foundation.

ICL launches its Vendor Accreditation scheme, which is subsequently used as a benchmark by the Department of Trade and Industry.

Survey of computer users in France perceives ICL mainframes as best in the world (for second consecutive year).

Site receptionist receives Gold Excellence award at ceremony in Southern France for providing exemplary service to external visitors and staff alike.

Continuous quality improvement now much more integrated into normal business. Previous initiatives continue and are improved (e.g. local Quality Management Teams, Graduate induction with quality theme, Corrective Action, training development and delivery, BS5750/ISO9001 registration, senior management Quality Improvement Teams, Joint (with customer) Quality Management Teams, internal audits, process control, business metrication, quality awareness events, management led action teams, etc., etc., etc.).

Product quality continues to improve – the "Software Factory" implementation improves the processes of software development. The development of the SX range of computers has more process controls and more quality checkpoints built in than any other development in the past.

Customer satisfaction with SX is notably higher than for any previous mainframe introduced by ICL.

The 1990 all-staff Opinion Survey indicates that some managers and staff have gained the impression that "We've stopped doing quality now." This is because quality management is now integrated into normal business and is not being "sold" as something special. Consequently, the need for managers to demonstrate continuing and increasing commitment to Total Quality is paramount. In 1987/8/9 managers had successfully secured buy-in from staff and convinced them that they were serious, they now need to ensure that staff do not become disillusioned. To support this, an initiative to give the first "mid-life kick" to the quality improvement drive is developed.

1991

HPT energy cost reduction project saves in excess of £200,000 per annum on one site alone. Lessons learned communicated throughout ICL.

Independent consultants audit staff restaurant operations and declare that it offers highest standards and best value for money. Customers routinely eat there too.

Focus moves to externally visible improvements as well as internal process improvements. Many organisations now use HPT as a benchmark to emulate. Academic institutions start to approach HPT for advice, guidance and case studies.

The ideas and experience from other organisations and other opinion leaders throughout the world are adopted and built in to HPT's training and education programmes.

ICL achieves company-wide ISO 9001 registration in the UK. Seventeen European operations are registered.

Internationally, operations in Hong Kong and Singapore are also registered.

An all staff Customer Care programme is designed in HPT.

1992

Customer Care training, education and workshops for all staff delivered in Q1. Each group identified between 3 and 5 realistic projects to be implemented throughout the year. By year-end 49 projects are completed. Each project was designed to exceed customer expectations.

ICL sets new goals:

— To be a household name for quality and Customer Care
— To be the best of the best
— To be the world's leading systems and service brand.

European Foundation for Quality Management's EQA self-assessment process is launched (cf. Baldrige in USA).

Customer Care support charter is launched, making response times to incidents more predictable.

Independent customer satisfaction surveys all show improvements.

Telephone responsiveness project yields order of magnitude improvement in responsiveness and customer satisfaction.

A customer visits programme, designed to allow direct personal contact between customers and non-customer facing technical staff, is developed. Within the first three years (1992/3/4) approximately 100 "back-room" staff had visited a customer site for a day to learn and share information. In addition, within the period 1992/3, 320 customer visits to HPT had taken place. Each visit involved an average of ten customer staff and five HPT staff.

Series 39 wins Gold for "Best corporate computer" in *Computing* magazine's excellence awards.

1993

ICL wins its third National Training Award for Customer Care training, education and workshops.

ICL 1992 results show profitability performance significantly better than all major competitors.

European Foundation for Quality Management self-assessment approach adopted throughout HPT and being used as an improvement driver both strategically and in local teams.

"Delta" system (for identifying and dealing with thousands of small improvement suggestions by everyone) is launched. Independent surveys show continuing improvements in customer perception.

HPT wins Queen's Award for technical achievement for Series 39 SX systems.

ICL becomes the first IT company to be accredited as an "Investor in People" – HPT was a reference site.

HPT creates a skills database of all staff to facilitate strategic organisation planning and development.

Manchester Business School develops a 3-week duration advanced management appreciation course for the Ministry of Defence aimed at senior officers from the three armed services. It provides a detailed insight into the workings of senior management within the best of civilian industry. HPT was invited, as the only external company, to develop and deliver a 1-day module in Managing Continuous Improvement and Customer Care for this course. This was delivered 3 times in 1993 and 5 times in 1994.

Series 39 wins second Gold for "Best corporate computer" in *Computing* magazine's excellence awards.

1994

The HPT board-level Quality and Customer Care Steering Team evolved into "The Business Excellence Team." They appointed a full-time Business Excellence Programme Manager to lead and oversee the whole-sale adoption of the EFQM's Business Excellence model as a tool for continuous improvement and to lead the development of a submission document for external assessment by the British Quality foundation (BQF).

HPT prepares its submission for assessment by the British Quality Foundation as a candidate for a UK Quality Award; and calls upon a team of internal and external assessors for a "dry run" to validate progress and attainments.

ICL's large systems manufacturing operation wins the EFQM European Quality Award.

HPT invests £110,000 in the development and delivery of a one-day sales, commercial and financial awareness course for all senior staff, both technical and managerial.

HPT was used as a benchmark for the implementation of ISO9001 by a visiting group of senior managers from General Motors Electromotive Division in Chicago (not a customer) who concluded that HPT was "world's best practice".

Series 39 wins third Gold for "Best corporate computer" in *Computing* magazine's excellence awards.

1995

HPT Wins the BQF UK Quality Award.

1996

The author leaves ICL.

Additional Statistics Over Period of Case Study

HPT maintains a population of approximately 90 trained ISO9001 auditors. HPT maintains a population of approximately 20 trained BQF assessors. Approximately 20% of HPT staff are members of professional bodies – notably the British Computer Society and the Institute of Electrical Engineers. Approximately half of these have "Chartered Engineer" status and some are Fellows (including the MD himself).

The 1-day "Managing Continuous Improvement and Customer Care" course for customers (developed in 1987) was, during this case study, delivered to more than 25 external organisations, not just customers, including: the DSS, the Inland Revenue, British Telecommunications plc, Price Waterhouse, The University of Manchester Institute of Science and Technology, the executive board of the British Computer Society, GCHQ and Cumbria County Council.

As well as quality management standards, HPT has maintained accreditation to five Open Systems Interconnect standards, two Open Systems X/Open standards and the MOD "B1" security standard.

HPT staff absenteeism rate averages 1.9% against national norm of 3.6%.

Staff-initiated departures from the company averages approximately 2% against a norm for companies employing more than 1,000 people of 11.7%.

HPT has had no days lost through industrial action during the period of this case study.

HPT invests approximately 3.6 days of training per person per year and has an annual training budget of approximately £600,000. (These figures do not include on-the-job training and personal development.)

Between 1993 and 1995 HPT raised or donated equipment

to local charities with a combined value of approximately £51,000.

During the period of the case study, electronic mail reduced paper consumption by 30%. While 45% of the 169 tons of paper used in 1994 was recycled.

ACKNOWLEDGEMENTS

I owe thanks to the many leaders, directors, managers and staff who have so graciously allowed me to see their organisations and how they have made the subject their own. In particular ICL. For it was here that I first started learning, then later developing, and then leading and teaching the management of change: wholesale change – to products, services, processes and to culture. From ICL, I thank, especially, Mike Warke. Mike bullied, goaded, encouraged and provided the necessary "ear-ache" to make me write this book and the various courses I developed on the subject. (Obviously he has no fear of mistakes!)

From the world of manufacturing and from the board room, I thank Tom Ainscough. Tom is a leader who constantly challenges conventional wisdom in business and expects (nay demands) that his people do the same. I have been privileged to serve as a consultant to some of his companies, and while he is as demanding as the very devil, his integrity is constant and people come first. In my experience Tom is one of only a tiny number of top managers who doesn't fake it! His personal motto is that progress is only made by being unreasonable. Tom "Thinks Change".

Finally, I thank Yvonne and our children Sarah and Mathew. I do not mention them here for all the usual boring things for which authors thank their families – though they did all that stuff too. Instead, I thank them for something much more important. I thank them for being irreverent. For it was irreverence that served as my check and balance on common sense. Without it, I would have made many simple ideas complicated, and, without an occasional well timed prick to my ego, I would have taken many ideas, and myself, too seriously.

I sincerely hope that you have enjoyed this book, and that it has given you a few ideas. But I hope too that you have read it with irreverence. Nothing that it says is absolute fact and no idea it expresses is a rule for success. "Think Change" means just that.

You need change, so you must think.

INDEX

In the same series

PRESENTATIONS
The Right Way To Make Effective Presentations

J Stuart Williams has given hundreds of presentations all over the world, for sales, technical and training purposes. He'll help you to prepare thoroughly, speak with confidence, emphasise the key points with visual aids and control your audience so that you always give an *effective* presentation.

THE RIGHT WAY TO WRITE REPORTS

A good report summarises the facts clearly, draws the correct conclusions, and gives the right recommendations for future action. With Steve Gravett's help *you* will be able to compile reports which are clear, succinct, accurate, fair and well written.

HANDLING PUBLICITY THE RIGHT WAY

Publicity is the key to selling your product or promoting your cause. Here journalist and media training consultant John Venables shows how it can be used to best effect. He'll give you the skills and knowledge you need to attract public attention if you want to be in the limelight – and how to cope if you don't!

Uniform with this book

RIGHT WAY
PUBLISHING POLICY

HOW WE SELECT TITLES

RIGHT WAY consider carefully every deserving manuscript. Where an author is an authority on his subject but an inexperienced writer, we provide first-class editorial help. The standards we set make sure that every **RIGHT WAY** book is practical, easy to understand, concise, informative and delightful to read. Our specialist artists are skilled at creating simple illustrations which augment the text wherever necessary.

CONSISTENT QUALITY

At every reprint our books are updated where appropriate, giving our authors the opportunity to include new information.

FAST DELIVERY

We sell **RIGHT WAY** books to the best bookshops throughout the world. It may be that your bookseller has run out of stock of a particular title. If so, he can order more from us at any time – we have a fine reputation for ''same day'' despatch, and we supply any order, however small (even a single copy), to any bookseller who has an account with us. We prefer you to buy from your bookseller, as this reminds him of the strong underlying public demand for **RIGHT WAY** books. Readers who live in remote places, or who are house-bound, or whose local bookseller is uncooperative, can order direct from us by post.

FREE

If you would like an up-to-date list of all **RIGHT WAY** titles currently ~~available~~, please send a stamped self-addressed envelope to ~~RIGHT~~ WAY BOOKS, BRIGHTON ROAD, ~~LOWER KINGSW~~OOD, TADWORTH, SURREY, KT20 6TD, U.K. ~~or se~~e at www.right-way.co.uk